The Book of Deer

And its Place in History

BY

Mary W. Melville

Published by Chalimar Publishing

For the Book of Deer Project

www.bookofdeer.co.uk, info@bookofdeer.co.uk

Find us on Facebook - Book of Deer Project

Printed by Peters Design & Print,

16 High St,

Turriff AB53 4DT

ISBN 978-1-3999-2259-3

Contents

Preface
An Appreciation of the Book of Deer

I cannot recall my first encounter with the "Book of Deer". Somehow, I seem to have been aware if its existence for quite some time. My real interest, however, was kindled when undertaking a short course in local history held at the Elphinstone Institute at Aberdeen University. One of the modules concentrated on the coming of Christianity to the Buchan area of Scotland. Two essays were requisite as part of the course, and I chose to investigate the Book of Deer as one of the topics.

It is not an exaggeration to say that once having become more knowledgeable about the manuscript, I was totally captivated by the amazing workmanship carried out by the holy men of the time as well as the contents on the written page. Not only the fact that scribes had lovingly written and illustrated the extracts of the Gospels, the Visitation for the Sick and the Apostles' Creed, but that such a revered book should be seen at the time as an appropriate place to record grants of lands to the holy community in which it was kept. The story of the foundation of the Monastery (believed to be late 6th or early 7th century) although written centuries later seemed so real and the final entry by the scribe himself is so poignant.

The study of the languages used within the folds and the names of the local rulers of the time as well as the place-names and landmarks mentioned make this little book an item priceless beyond words. It is not an exaggeration to say that the history of the Buchan area and the way of life of the populace would never have been uncovered. Even the whole history of Scotland may have been quite bereft of some detail if this book had not survived to this day.

The following account is not 'the last word' in the history of the object, neither is it a full and academic appreciation of the delights contained therein, no it is a more personal reading of the information available and has my own interpretation of the evidence.

The Book of Deer is in the safe-keeping of Cambridge University Library and even the tale of how it became to be housed therein is a cause for speculation.

The selected events within the Pictish era are given with the aim of placing the construction of the book within a wider framework. The possible route of the coming of Christianity to the Buchan area helps to gives the background to the early development of places of worship and finally the description and content of the book is described within. A further chapter explores what is known of the monastery at Turriff and the story ends with a review of the efforts being made to find the exact location of the monastery.

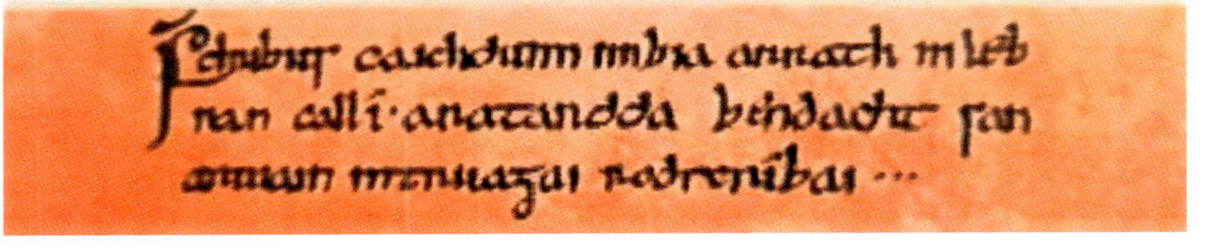

Scribe's Final Entry

Translates as :

"Be it on the conscience of anyone who reads this splendid little book that they say a prayer for the soul of the wretch who wrote it"[1]

Mary W. Melville
February 2022

Reference

1 **Kellock, A.** (c. 2010). *This Splendid Little Book*. The Book of Deer Project : Mintlaw (Leaflet)

Acknowledgements

This book would not have been as complete without the generous permission of Cambridge University Library who allowed the reproduction of their illustrations from the Book of Deer to be included within these pages.

I must express my gratitude to those who have willingly given me critical appraisals and invaluable support throughout the conception and development of this book: Stuart Donald, Maureen and Alexander Crawford, Lesley Jennings, Sandy Ritchie, Dorothy Chapman and Isobel Burnside, Corinne Cox, Keith Martin, Vi May, Murray Martin, David George (of Peters Design and Print) and especially to Joyce Brown for devoting much of their time and effort during the evolution of this volume. All have given me advice, guidance, support and encouragement throughout the process of conveying the thoughts and theories which are expressed throughout this book. To them I will be eternally grateful.

This book is dedicated to

The Book of Deer Project (SCIO)

Scottish Charity No: SCO30656

The proceeds from this book will go towards funding the future aims of the "Project".

Introduction

Categorised as "An Irish Pocket Gospel Book", The Book of Deer is a vellum manuscript measuring approximately the size of a postcard. It contains extracts of the first three Gospels of the New Testament and all of the fourth Gospel of St. John written in Latin. The book is decorated with figures and patterns. It is thought the gospels were written in the first half of the 10th century.

However, it is not the Gospels, nor the illustrations, which make the "Splendid Little Book" so important. It is the use of the native language of Scottish Gaelic which makes it so precious and unique. The book in fact contains the oldest records of Gaelic writings known in Scotland.

The bulk of these Gaelic insertions, added to the book during the 12th century in the margins of the first few pages, are records of lands granted to the clerics of the Monastery of Deer. They provide names of specific locations and landmarks (some identifiable even today) which gives the book its name and places the book indisputably in the Monastery of Deer at that time.

[1]

It is thought the Monastery of Deer was in existence in the late 6th or early 7th century and the story of the foundation of the monastery by St Columba and St

Drostan is in fact the first of the Gaelic writings in the book, although scribed much later.

Deer or more precisely, Old Deer, is a parish in the Buchan area of north Aberdeenshire in the north-east of Scotland.

The Book of Deer Project is a charitable foundation which was set up with the intention of promoting the Book of Deer in the local area as well as trying to discover the exact location of the monastery itself. To that end several archaeological digs have been carried out in and around Old Deer. Most recent excavations have centred around the grounds of the Cistercian Abbey of Deer which is close by. The abbey is a later structure, founded in AD 1219 by a leader of Norman ancestry, William Comyn, Earl of Buchan. The ruins of the Abbey are cared for by Historic Environment Scotland.

[2]

1 Map by L. J. Brown

2 **Kellock, A.** (c. 2010). *This Splendid Little Book.* The Book of Deer Project : Mintlaw (Leaflet)

1

The Picts and Deer

THE PICTISH TIMELINE RELATING TO THE BOOK OF DEER

As noted above, it is claimed that the major Biblical portion of the Book of Deer was written in 10th century Caledonia, Caledonia being the name given by the Romans to an area of north Britain beyond the frontier of their empire.[1] The inhabitants, whom they named as "The Picts" are said to be the indigenous people of Scotland, certainly of the north of Scotland. Their history is long but poorly documented. In fact, "anything about the Picts must be highly speculative. The rarity of recorded accounts of that mysterious people, and the fact that their few remaining inscriptions are almost entirely indecipherable means that anything about their political history ... depends on deductions from an exiguous collection of references by foreigners".[2]

The much-discredited paper "De Situ Albanie", part of the *Poppleton Manuscripts* tells the story of a king, Albanectus, also known as Cruithne, son of Brutus, who was the father of seven sons. On his death each son inherited a province of the Kingdom The provinces in Pictland are identified as:

- Cait - Caithness and Sutherland
- Fidach - Inverness and the west
- Fortriu - Moray and Ross
- Cé - Mar with Buchan
- Circinn - Angus and the Mearns
- Fotla - Atholl
- Fib – Fife[3]

Provinces of Pictland [4]

It was the Venerable Bede (AD 672/3 – 735) who first recorded the division of Pictavia into the North and South in his *Ecclesiastical History of The English People (AD 731),* the natural dividing line being the Grampian mountains.[5] The first four provinces of Cait, Fidach, Fortriu and Cé were in the territory of the Northern Picts, whilst the remaining provinces of Circinn, Fotla and Fib were inhabited by the Southern Picts.[6] Each province became a mormaerdom and are currently viewed by some scholars as kingdoms.

The Picts are first recorded by the Romans under Agricola, who in AD 80, invaded Scotland reaching as far as the rivers Forth and Clyde. Three years later they extended into northern Scotland and confronted and defeated the natives at the Battle of Mons Graupius.[7] Thereafter the Romans built a line of forts between Loch Lomond and Stonehaven with the object of containing the Picts to the north. The consequence being that the northern Picts became isolated from those in the south.

Unfortunately, Cé, the territory of modern Buchan and Mar in which Deer is situated, is poorly documented. Noble and Evans, when discussing Cé, state: "Cé is found in the title of two stories in the 10th and 11TH centuries medieval Irish tale lists". They add "...in addition, a tale about a person called Frigriu, this character is described as 'the artificer of Cruthmag Cé' ".[8] This story is said to be more fable than fact, although there is evidence for the existence of at least some of these. However, it is claimed that "Cé is a rendering of the pictish Ci which refers to a Dog Clann. This is not a reference to any old dog, but rather to the war hounds which the Picts of those days did indeed use".[9] This is remarkably interesting since the one-time rulers of Cé were the Clann of the Dog and, in addition, a number of drawings of dogs are to be found in the Book of Deer. These facts will be returned to later when exploring the Book of Deer itself.

The Romans began building Hadrian's Wall along the line between the rivers Solway and Tyne around AD 122.[10] Later, c. AD 142, the Antonine Wall was erected between the rivers Forth and Clyde.[11] Around AD 383 the Romans started to withdraw from the north of Britain.[12] The Scots, a tribe who originated in the north of Ireland, started invading, raiding, then settling the west of the country. They went on to found the Kingdom of Dal Riada consisting of the lands of Antrim in north-east Ireland and the lands of Argyll and the Inner Hebrides.[13]

It is believed that St. Ninian, a Romanised Briton born c. AD 367 and a Christian, built the first Christian church in the Isle of Whithorn (now in Dumfries and Galloway) where he began his teachings.[14] It was his pupils who then began to spread the Christian message eastward and northward to the Picts.[15] Ninian died in AD 432.

By AD 500 the Scots had settled in the west coast in Dal Riada with Fergus Mor, King of the Scots, fighting the Picts in the east and the Britons of Strathclyde to the south in order to expand his territory.[16] Soon after this there is evidence that Christianity was spreading northwards to the Southern Pictland territories of Fife and Angus.[17] At the same time, around AD 520, Saints Drostan, Colm, Fergus and Modan settled in the Buchan area with the aim of spreading Christianity to the inhabitants of Buchan and beyond and the monastery of Deer becomes established.[18] By the end of the 6th century Bridei, King of the Picts from AD 554 to 584, obtained overall rulership of the Pictish Kingdoms in Northern Pictland and Christianity had become the established religion.[19]

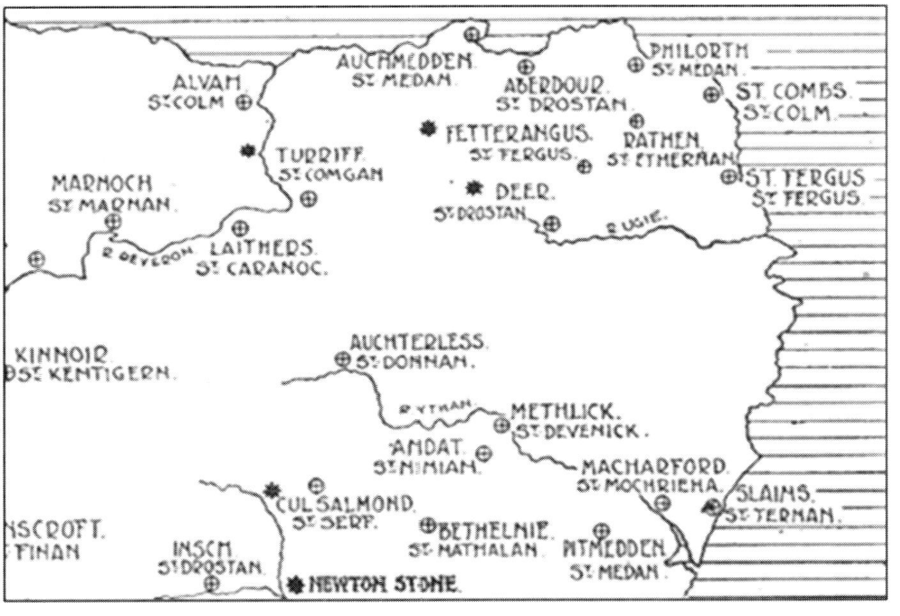

Early Christian Settlements in the North-East.[20]

In AD 790 the Vikings carried out their first attack on Iona and by AD 839 there was the start of Northern Pictland being repeatedly raided.[21] By AD 843 Kenneth MacAlpin had inherited the kingship of both the Scots of Dal Riada and Pictland and the Kingdom of Alba was founded. For safety against the Viking raiders Kenneth MacAlpin moved his court to Scone.[22] At the same time the official language became Gaelic which inevitably led to the decline of the use of the Pictish language.[23] The Picts did not disappear but gradually were integrated into the population. They left behind a legacy of carved standing stones.

PICTISH STANDING STONES

Probably the most abundant record of the Picts today are their carved standing stones. Numerous studies and many scholarly articles have been written about them over time.

In *The Early Christian Monuments of Scotland* (1903) J. Romilly Allen and Joseph Anderson first classified Pictish stones into three groups.

CLASS I

Unworked stones with symbols only incised. There is no cross on either side. Class I stones date back to the 6th, 7th and 8th century.

CLASS II

Stones of more or less rectangular shape with a large cross and symbol(s) on one or both sides. The symbols, as well as Christian motifs, are carved in relief and the cross with its surroundings is filled with designs. Class II stones date from the 8th and 9th century.

CLASS III

These stones feature no idiomatic Pictish symbols. The stones can be cross-slabs, recumbent gravemarkers, free-standing crosses, and composite stone shrines. They originate in the 8th or 9th century. Historic Scotland describes this class as "too simplistic" and says "Nowadays this is not considered a useful category. A surviving fragment may belong to a monument that did include Christian imagery".[24]

In an article dated 2018, Dr Gordon Noble, Head of Archaeology at the University of Aberdeen states: "According to the new findings, the smaller, simpler symbols of Class II do not represent a later form of carving at all – instead, they date to the 3rd to 4th centuries AD, while the more elaborate Class I carvings appear to be of a later date, most likely from the 6th to early 7th century AD". Then "by the 9th or 10th century, the symbols seem to have disappeared completely, with the emergence of the kingdom of Alba and development of a new language".[25] However, even if the Allan and Anderson classification is seen as too simplistic it is still frequently used today.

Distribution of Class I and Class II stones.[26]

It is claimed that around AD 710 crosses began to be carved into Pictish stones. The lost stone of Deer which once stood in the grounds of Deer Abbey, the Cistercian ruled monastery founded by William Comyn, Earl of Buchan in AD 1219, is likely to have been an early Class 1 stone with a cross later carved on the reverse. Stuart describes it as a "whinstone. The cross was incised on the face of the pillar, and on the obverse was the now well-known, though yet undeciphered semi-lunar hieroglyphic".

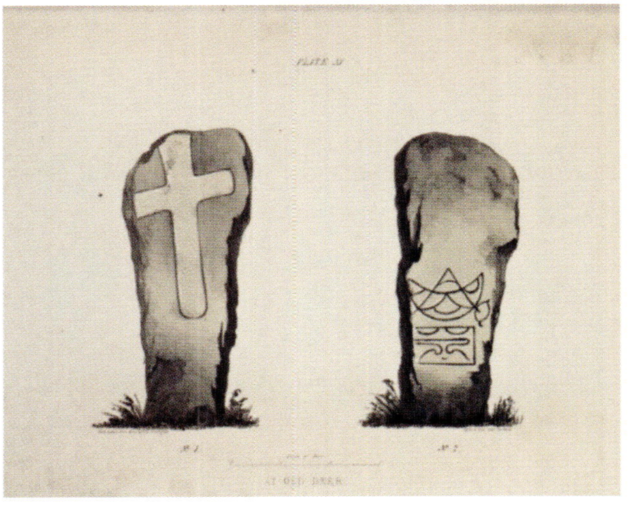

[27]

Store of Deer

Stuart also recorded that it had been located at the west end of the old Abbey Church although it is speculated that this may not have been the original position considering it was much older than the abbey. However, by AD 1854 it had disappeared around the same time as the site was being cleared by the owner, Admiral George Ferguson of Pitfour.

When describing the antiquities within the Parish of Deer in AD 1795 Mr George Cruden gives the following description: "At a distance of about 500 yards (from the stone circle on the Hill of Parkhouse (or Aikey Brae)), on the north east side of the same hill, where (was), not long ago the ruins of a small village supposed to have been the residence of the druids. A number of little yards were to be seen all around it, one of which still retains a superior verdure (lush green vegetation) and serves now to show the spot where the village once stood. It consisted of 50 or 60 mossy huts, from 6 to 12 feet square, irregularly huddled together; hence it got the name of the *bourachs*. The walls were built of stone and clay; the floors were paved with stones. A farmer in the neighbourhood, about 20 years ago, applied the stones, which were all of a similar size, to erect inclosures (sic). In removing the rubbish he found a cylindrical stone, like a small mill-stone; probably part of the *qurarn,* or hand-mill, anciently used in this country for grinding corn. Two circular huts, containing some ashes, seem to have been corn-kilns".[28] There is no longer any evidence of this settlement.

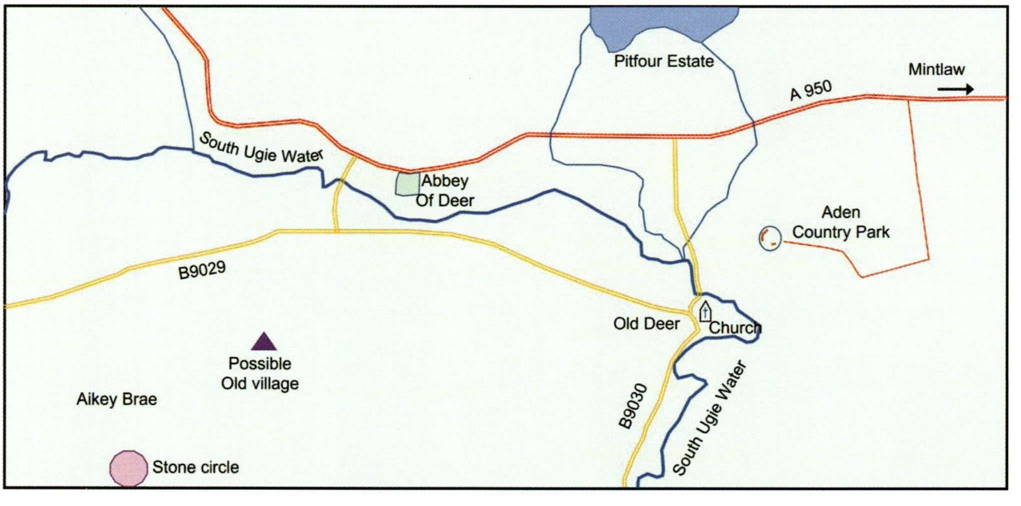

Stone Circle bottom left and Abbey of Deer top centre[29]

The Book of Deer Gospels are thought to have been written sometime between AD 850-1000.[30] Where it was prepared and written is uncertain although there is no evidence that the book was not written in the Monastery of Deer. What is sure is that the scribe was a native Pict both by the quality of his copying of the Latin text and the colophon written at the end of the book in his native Gaelic. What is certain is that when the Land Grants were recorded in the Book of Deer, around the early 12th century, it was in the hands of the occupants of the monastery.

RULERS OF ALBA

Around the time the gospels were written in the Book of Deer, the King of Alba was Constantin II, the son of Aed who reigned for 40 years from AD 900 to 943. During his kingship his army is said to have defeated the Norse raid on Dunkeld and later again at Strathearn.[31] The Pictish Chronicle recounts that, in the 6th year of his rule, King Constantin and his son, Bishop Cellach, vowed that the laws and teachings of the faith and the rights of the churches and gospels were to be protected.[32]

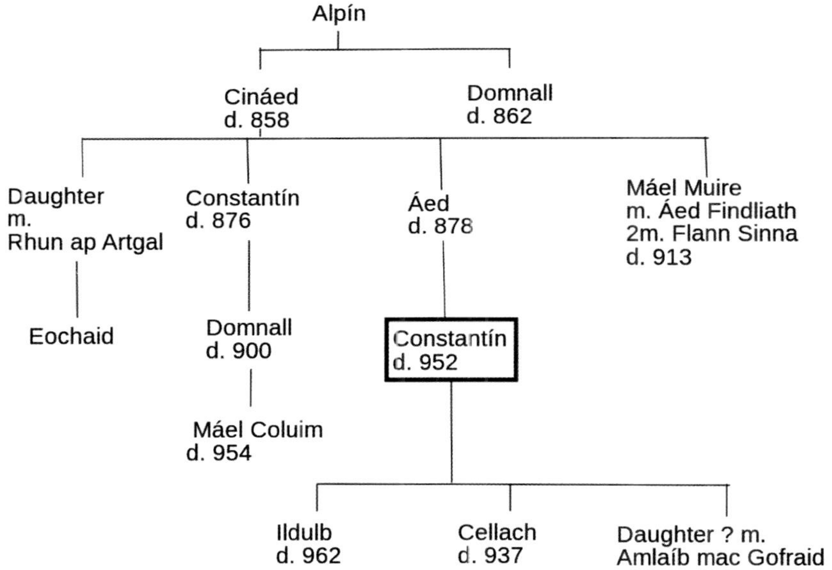

[33]

Chart showing the relationship of Constantin II to the Alpin Family

Later there was a battle in Duinbrunde in the north of England where the Albans were defeated, and his son Cellach was killed. Constantin II reached old age and infirmity which led to his abdication and he entered the monastery at St. Andrews.[34]

Constantin II's kingship was inherited by his cousin Donald's (Domnall) son Malcolm I (Mael Coluim), who was killed two years later at Fetteresso by rebels from Moray.[35] A period of hostilities between two rivals for kingship followed until Kenneth II. He made peace with King Edgar of England by swearing loyalty to him. He was murdered at Fettercairn in AD 995 by a vengeful rival. He was followed by his nephew Kenneth III, then his son Malcolm II then, in turn, Malcolm II's grandson Duncan I (AD 1034 – 40), followed by Macbeth (AD 1040 – 57), then by Duncan I's son Malcolm III – Malcolm Canmore, (AD 1057-93).[36]

By the 11th century the different territories within Pictland were under the rule of a mormaer, or sub-king who was only answerable to the king himself. He was assisted by the toiseach, or officer of the state.[37]

The early Mormaers of Buchan:

Unknowns

Possibly Cainnech (*fl.* (flourished) early 12th century)

Gartnait (*fl.* after AD 1131)

Éva (Éua) ingen Garnait (*fl.* AD 1174) married Colbán (*fl.* AD 1174)

Fergus (*d. before* AD 1214)

Marjory daughter of Fergus, married William Comyn, Justiciar of Scotia and Warden of Moray (d. AD 1233)

Alexander Comyn (d. AD 1289)[38]

Some of these Mormaers names are mentioned in the Gaelic entries in the Book of Deer which were written into the book in the 12th century.

Malcolm III (Malcolm Canmore) married Ingeborg, widow of Earl Thorfinn of Orkney and they had two sons, Duncan and Donald, who probably died before their father as neither became king. After her death he married Margaret, daughter of Edward the Athelring and refugee from the wars of William the Conqueror. She was a pious and devout Christian whose beliefs in certain rites differed from that practiced by the Celtic Church. They had eight children, among them was Edward, Edmund, Edgar, Alexander and David.

Malcolm died with his eldest son Edward at a battle with the Norman English in AD 1093. Margaret died three days later.[39] She was canonised by Pope Innocent IV in

AD 1250 in recognition of her personal holiness, fidelity to the Roman Catholic Church, work for ecclesiastical reform, and charity.[40]

[41]

Margaret of Scotland
in stained glass at Aldeburgh

Three of her sons became King of Scotland, Edgar AD 1097-1107, Alexander AD 1107-24 and David I AD 1124-53.[42] The final entry in the Book of Deer, written in Latin, is a record of a charter from King David I.

2

How Christianity came to Buchan

THE MONASTERY OF DEER

It was Mark Twain who is credited with the adage "Never let the truth stand in the way of a good story".[1] The tale of the origins of the Monastery of Deer would certainly conform to this statement. The key to defining an early medieval monastery often lies in its proximity to towns and people, as it weighed solitary and tedious meditative practices above all else. Though the early monasteries of Britain and Ireland were not as sophisticated as those of the east, by the 9th century they became highly organised. [2]

One of the most elusive structures in Buchan must be the Monastery of Deer. There is no doubt that myths and legends have grown around it almost since Christianity arrived in the north-east of Scotland. Furthermore, every claim made about the Monastery's history can be disputed. Was there only one monastery? Who were the founders? Did Columba really land at Aberdour Shore? A monastery is defined by Simpson as "collections of buildings, cemeteries and working areas within an enclosure ... grafted on to the existing network of regional, tribally based sees".

A concept of a Pictish monastery, its structure and organisation, is described as:-

> *"A busy little community where manuscripts were read and copied and where schools were established to spread religion and civilization among the rude inhabitants".* It goes on — *"We may readily picture our little community, with its group of wooden or wattle huts, its smithy, its barns and byres, its bakery, its kiln for corn-dying and its little heather-thatched church of uncemented stone—all enclosed by a fencible dry-built wall and earthen bank, and surrounded by the neat patches of cultivated soil upon which the holy brethren worked".*

It Continues:

> *"Most of the inhabitants would be laymen, exempt from the heavy duties of religious service, and wholly taken up with the practical work and manual labour of the community. The religious brethren, or monks proper were grouped into three classes—the Seniors, who were old men past active work and rich in holiness, the Working Brethren, on whom the main burden of the missionary and education work of the monastery was cast, and the juniors, or novices under instruction".* And *"The system of devotional exercises was very severe".*

Their garb or mode of dress and living conditions is also described as being of:

> *"The simplest form, consisting of a shirt reaching to the heels, and an upper garment with hood and sleeves; shoes of hide, and a white surplice for use at festivals. All classes lived with the greatest austerity, sleeping on beds of stone, or boards covered with straw, each monk having his own cell or hut".* There were also retreats *"where the holy brethren would withdraw on occasions for solitary meditation".*[3]

4

Pictish stone showing a monk carrying a book

The monks would travel some distances with the aim of spreading the gospel and generally setting the standards of a Christian way of life. It is likely that on these occasions they would carry with them a small pocket book containing gospel messages and religious rites, the "Book of Deer" being an example.

"Folio 3 of the Book of Deer (*Leabhar Dhèir*) contains a continuation of the Latin Gospel According to St. Matthew and a Scottish Gaelic account of the foundation of the Monastery of Deer by SS. Columba and Drostan."[5]

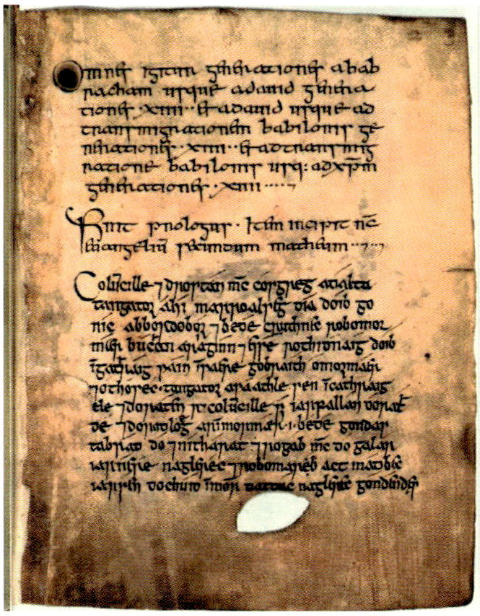

Folio 3r

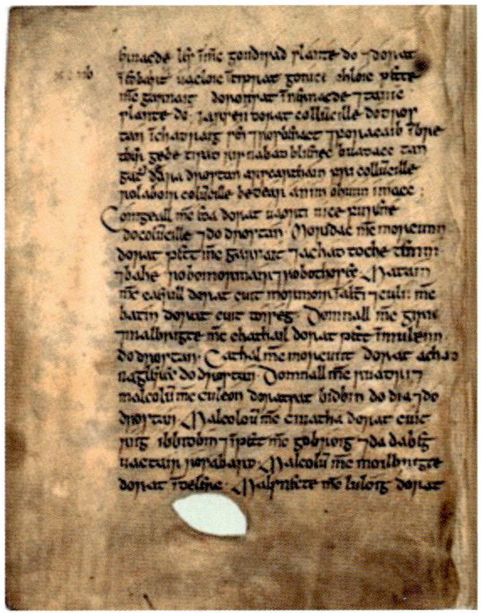

Folio 3v

This reads: *"Columba and Drostán son of Coscrach, his disciple, came from Iona, as God guided them, to Aberdour; and Bede the Pict was mormaer of Buchan on their arrival; and it is he who bestowed on them that monastery, in freedom till Doomsday from mormaer and toíseach. They came after that to the other monastery, and it pleased Columba, for it was full of the grace of God. And he begged the mormaer, that is, Bede, that he should give it to them, and he did not. And a son of his took a sickness, after the clerics had been refused, and was all but dead. Thereupon the mormaer went to beseech the clerics that they should make a prayer on behalf of the boy, that health might come to him; and he gave to them land as a grant from Cloch in Tiprat as far as Cloch Peitte Meic-Garnait. They made the prayer, and health came to him. Thereupon Columba gave Drostán that monastery, and blessed it, and left the curse that whoever should go against it should not be full of years or of success. Drostán's tears [déra] came as he was parting from Columba. Columba said, 'Let Deer be its name from this on'."*[6]

This entry in the Book of Deer implies that the Saints were initially granted land for a monastery at New Aberdour and it is recorded that excavations carried out in AD 1951 at Dundarg Castle revealed "some kind of church building under the medieval castle ruins".[7] However the saints requested land for another monastery further inland.

The record in the Book of Deer describing how St. Columba and St. Drostan founded the monastery at Deer is well known and accepted as true. But is this so? It is a fact that the history of any war is usually written by the victors and thus must be judged as biased. The story of the founding of the monastery of Deer must be seen in a similar light.

Certainly, when seeking the earliest written records about the first millennium AD there are few entries to consult. Those who have cited works frequently quote the same sources thus conferring on the authors a degree of authenticity and reliability which does nothing but serve to perpetuate their assertions, true or false. Today, little or no facts are available regarding some early events, while others have so many claims made about them that they cannot all be true.

THE ROMANS AND THE PICTS

The Northern Picts must be viewed as aboriginal tribes of the north of Scotland, each tribe having its own king. It is claimed that they are first mentioned in AD 43 when it is stated that the "King of Orkney" was part of a delegation to visit the Roman Emperor Claudius after his army had invaded what was then southern Britain.[8]

In AD 80 Julius Agricola, the Roman Governor of Britain invaded Scotland and in AD 84 the Battle of Mons Graupius took place somewhere in Aberdeenshire. On defeating the Picts he built a line of forts between Loch Lomond and Stonehaven, in order to contain the Northern Picts, the Southern Picts occupying the lands south of the fortifications. In AD 105 the Romans recognised that the Picts were unconquerable and withdrew south. Hadrian's Wall was built c. AD 121. Soon after the Romans once again advanced north and the Antonine Wall was built c. AD 142. But by AD 170 they had retreated to behind Hadrian's Wall.

During the time of the Roman occupation of Britain, the Roman Empire had adopted Christianity as the state religion, beginning with the Emperor Constantin's decree of religious toleration, the Edict of Milan, in AD 314. Christian missionaries began making inroads into the beliefs of the Southern Pictish people beginning with St. Ninian,

(c. AD 360 – 432), a Briton who had travelled abroad to learn more about Christianity and study the teachings of St. Martin of Tours.[9]

The concept of monasticism originated in Egypt during the second half of the 3rd century. Before long, the idea spread throughout Christendom and arrived in Italy.

[10]

Martin of Tours (AD 316 – 372) was a Roman soldier who became a devout Christian and learned of the monastic way of life. He left the army and travelled around spreading the faith as he went. On settling in Gaul (France) he set up a small monastery attracting others to join him. He was appointed the Bishop of Tours but, on finding the way of life was not to his pleasing, in 372 he established a monastery at Marmoutier, outside the town, which attracted a substantial number of monks. The way of life was strict but familiar to an ex-soldier. The monks lived in a community, wore similar rough garments, ate, slept and prayed together and were celibate. They had nothing of their own, all possessions being communal. The monks participated in teaching, writing manuscripts and pioneering agricultural processes. Some monks were hermits living in isolation while others left the monastery to travel far with the aim of spreading the Gospel.[11] St Martin went on to be known as the "Father of Monasticism in Gaul", the first great leader of western monasticism as well as being adopted as a Patron Saint of France.[12]

[13]

Saint Martin of Tours

[14]

Saint Ninian

In AD 397, on Ninian's return to his home at Whithorn, an area located in the south-west of present-day Scotland, he built a church of stone (Candida Casa) and founded a monastery. Under St Ninian, Whithorn developed into a cathedral church, a title probably reflecting its status rather than its size.

The monastery became renowned as a centre of learning and was the origin of many of the missionaries who later converted Scotland to Christianity.[15]

The earliest mention of Ninian of Whithorn is in a short passage of *The Ecclesiastical History of the English People* by the Northumbrian monk Bede (AD 672—735), written c. 731.[16] Over time Ninian's followers spread their message to the east and northwards, gradually entering the lands of the Northern Picts.[17]

[18]

SAINTS DROSTAN, FERGUS, MEDAN AND COLM

Of these four saints, all followers of St. Ninian, whose presence in the Buchan area of north-east Scotland is acknowledged as generally belonging to the early 6th century (c. AD 500), the best know is Drostan. It is Drostan who is said to have been accompanied by three other saints in their efforts to evangelise the north-east. They were Fergus, Medan (or Modan) and Colm (or Colman).

It is claimed that "The influence of the missionary centre at Deer was enormous and it may be argued that with these workers, Christianity became firmly established across the north-east". Furthermore "Deer was, without doubt, one of the most important centres of Christian missionary work in Europe at the time, to compare with ease with any other".[19]

SAINT DROSTAN

Saint Drostan [21]

So far it has not been possible to determine at which British or Pictish school Drostan was trained. All that is authentic is that "he came off the sea at Aberdour" in northern Aberdeenshire and, after a time, went inland and settled his *muinntir (community) at Deer* under the sanction of the Pictish Mormaer of Buchan, Bede Cruithnech. Bede had at first been hostile to Drostan's settlement but came to accept his presence in time. The Buchan authorities give Drostan's dates as c. AD 500, whilst the date of his fellow missionary, St_Fergus, is given as "the beginning of the sixth age", c. AD 520. He is said to have travelled beyond Buchan to Moray in the west and as far north as Caithness and Orkney.[20] Towill quotes Knight's phrase "Drostan and his three" and states "This is interpreted as meaning Drostan with Colm, Medan and Fergus". He continues "Nothing is known of the lives of any of these figures except that they all left a great many place names in Aberdeenshire and the north-east".[22]

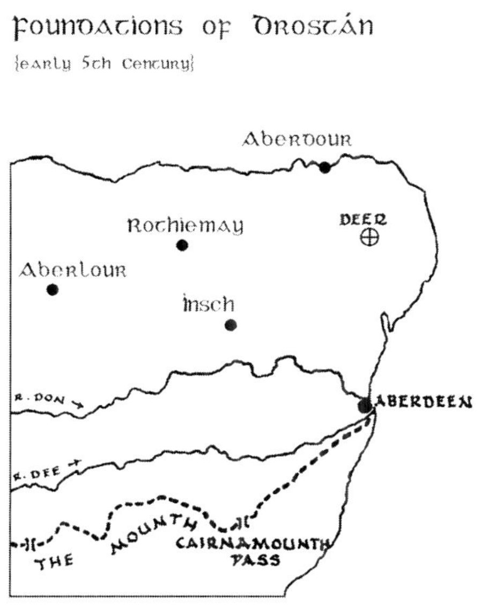

Foundations of St. Drostan [23]

SAINT FERGUS

Saint Fergus is altogether a more illusory figure. His name is claimed to be Pictish and it seems there may have been more than one saint with this name. Stories about him crop up in three main areas of Scotland. He is the patron saint of Wick and is said to have founded two churches in Caithness, which at the time was home to a Pictish kingdom. He is also associated with Aberdeenshire both via Saint Drostan and, it is said, by founding his own churches there. He is most notably remembered in the name of the village of St. Fergus.[24]

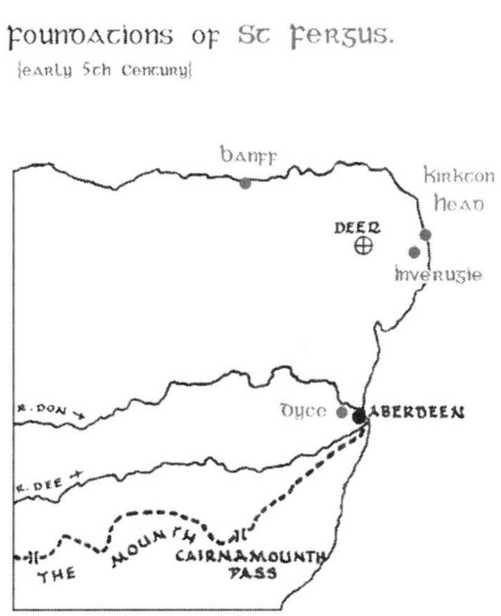

Foundations of St. Fergus [25]

SAINT MODAN (MEDAN)

It is claimed that "On the Links east of Fraserburgh a now vanished knoll was supposedly the location of a chapel founded by St Modan in the sixth century, which may have been the precursor of the old Kirk of Philorth. There were also some holy wells in the medieval parish of

Philorth, one of which was dedicated and named after the sixth century saint Modan".[26] He is described as "A bishop in great favour with King Couran about 503".[27] It is also recorded that when the 1910 extension of Fraserburgh's Kirkton cemetery was being laid out the workers came across the foundations of the old Kirk of Philorth along with the unique key to the door. The church was located partly outside and partly inside the oldest part of the cemetery. The chapel at Philorth, which was claimed to be connected to a monastery or "college" at Archyseipal in Phingask probably around Chapelhill and to another at Chapelton south of Pitblae, is said to be associated with Modan. The historic evidence for the existence of these chapels is cited by Murison and Noble when detailing local place names and their origins.[28] St Modan is nowadays the patron Saint of Fraserburgh. He is also associated with another chapel at Pitmeddan near Udny.

SAINT COLM

"We must turn our thoughts back to 'the start of the sixth age' and allow ourselves to dream of the sound of an ancient chant coming from within the tiny church at Deer to find our friend Colm. He had come with Drostan, Fergus and Medan to establish a Christian community amongst the Picts of Buchan as the sixth century dawned upon the rolling countryside."[29] St. Colm also travelled to Tain, Caithness and Orkney. It should be noted that Tain is close to the Tarbat peninsula, the location of Portmahomack monastery.

ST. COLUMBA, ST. COLMAN OR ST. COLM?

It is known that St. Columba - *Colm Cille*, was born in Ireland in AD 521, at the same time the four saints were settling in Buchan. However, Columba did not land at Iona with his twelve companions until AD 563. Furthermore, he did not speak the language of the north-east region. The assertion made is - that Colm is easily translated as Colm Cille and furthermore it is accepted that the legend in the Book of Deer was written in Old Irish script in the 12th century.

The explanation given is that by this time the Picts had been integrated with the Celtic Scots, around AD 843 under King Kenneth McAlpin, whose lineage is said to have been both Pictish and Celtic. The monks of the Monastery of Deer would have been descendants of many generations of the Picts and Scots by the time any of the Gaelic entries were made in the Book of Deer (c. late 11th or early 12th centuries). The first Gaelic entry in the Book of Deer, which recounts the story of Saints landing at

Aberdour shore replaces St Colm with St. Colm Cille (Columba), who would have bestowed more kudos and admiration on the event, the Irish St. Columba being the much more renowned of the two.

Another area for debate regarding the confusion of St. Colm and St. Columba is the relatively recent uncovering of the monastery at Portmahomack, a village located in the Tarbat peninsula. It is possible that St. Colman of Portmahomack could quite easily have sailed from the Buchan coast as St. Colm and landed at Portmahomack as St. Colman. This may have simply been due to dialect.

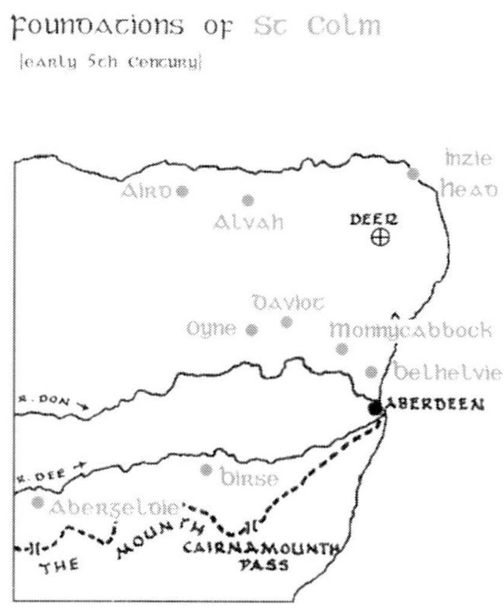

Foundations of St. Colm

in Buchan

30

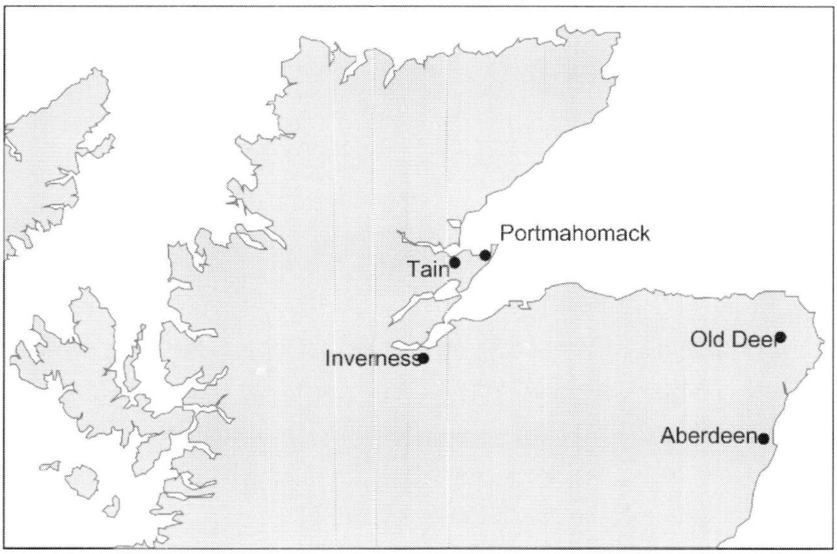

31

Map showing Portmahomack in relation to Old Deer

In AD 1994 archaeologists uncovered a Pictish monastery at Portmahomack, said to have dated from c. AD 550 (pre Columban). The church is dedicated to St. Colman or Colm, the saint from Buchan who is said to have travelled to Tain and beyond during his lifetime. The monastery has a burial ground with cist and head-support burials, a stone church, at least four monumental stone crosses and workshops making church plate and early Christian books.[32]

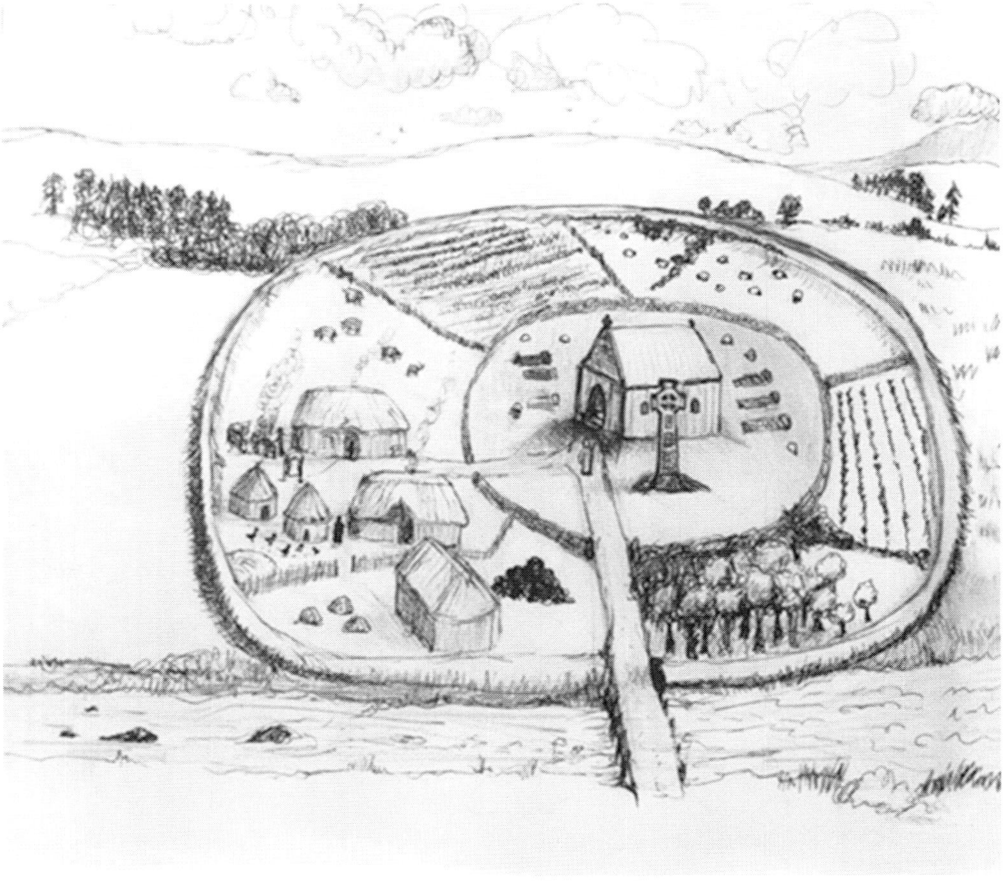

33

Artist's impression of a Pictish monastery by Lesley Jennings with kind permission

It is probable that St. Colm was the founder of the monastery but it has also been linked with St Columba. The first church built on the site of the current St. Colman's church is dated as being from the 8th century.[34]

A monastery would not have been built at once and remain unchanged thereafter. It is fair to claim that, like any other structure, monastic buildings would have evolved through time as the needs of the monks developed. The image of a circular enclosure, containing church, homes, burial ground and workshops seem to have evolved from the design of structures found in Ireland.

However, the monastery at Deer and that of Portmahomack are more likely to have been modelled on St. Ninian's Candida Casa, which in turn, would have been much influenced by the structures at Tours.

[35]

Papil Stone with four Pictish monks.

The association of "The Book of Deer" with the founders of the Monastery is very vague to say the least, but there can be no disputing that "this splendid little book", whether originating from the monastery of Deer or otherwise, was in the keeping of the monks of the monastery when King David I issued his 1153 Charter. The properties of this unique, precious, and historic book will now be explored.

3

The Book of Deer - The Gospels

1

Photograph by M. Melville at Cambridge University Library.

The Book of Deer is described by Cambridge University authors Patrick Zutshi and Paul Binski who record it as "a Gospel Book written in a hand that was current in the period c. 850-1000 and generally dated to the first half of the tenth century and it is widely regarded as the earliest manuscript produced in Scotland." They go on, "The manuscript belongs to the category of 'Irish pocket Gospel Books' produced for private use rather than for church services".

They add that the book itself consists of "86 folios of parchment measuring: height: 157 mm, width: 108 mm. the text occupying: 108 mm X 71 mm. Each page having 22-26 lines, ruled in hard point. It is bound in goatskin (Douglas Cockerell & Son, Letchworth, 1963), which replaced a sheepskin Bowtell-style binding of 18th-19th century, which is kept together with the manuscript".[2]

It is generally agreed that the original text was written by one scribe using insular half-uncial script, or more exactly "Irish majuscule": the most formal font of the period. The illustrations within are said to be by at least two illustrators.[3] There is no suggestion as to whether the script writer was one of the illustrators, but the artistry of his text cannot exclude the possibility.

The Book of Deer was written on several sections of parchment. Once the book was completed each section was assembled in order and sewn or bound together to make the complete book. A cover would have been constructed. possibly made of wood with a leather protective covering.[4]

THE GOSPELS AND OTHER RELIGIOUS CONTENT OF THE BOOK OF DEER

The Book of Deer was originally constructed and written in the 9th or 10th century. Thus, it must be kept in mind that the contents are not from today's Bible but of one transcribed from another of a much earlier period. Consequently, to better understand the biblical contents of the Book of Deer a short history of the origins of the books of the Gospel contained in the New Testament follows.

The synoptic writers (or those authors with similar stories), Matthew, Mark and Luke were the first to have their words recorded. Their Gospels are said to date from around AD 60 and are written in Greek. These three Gospels share a significant portion of the same content thus it is considered possible that each referred to the work of the others. They are considered to have been recorded using as much of the teachings of the preachers which could be recalled. As a result, a substantial amount of the information is shared. When the Gospels were written and in what order is a subject of much debate and is termed "The Synoptic Problem".[5]

The Gospel according to St John is of a later date (c. AD 96), and most of the contents differs from that of the previous books. "The first seventeen chapters for the most part, contain matter not found in the other gospels. The other chapters likewise contain many particulars not recorded by the other evangelists."[6]

The Codex Sinaiticus is one of the four oldest copies of the Bible, others being the Codex Vaticanus, the Codex Alexandrinus and the Codex Ephraemi Rescriptu. The Codex Sinaiticus was written around AD 360, making it well over 1600 years old. Written in Greek, it contains the oldest complete copy of the New Testament.[7]

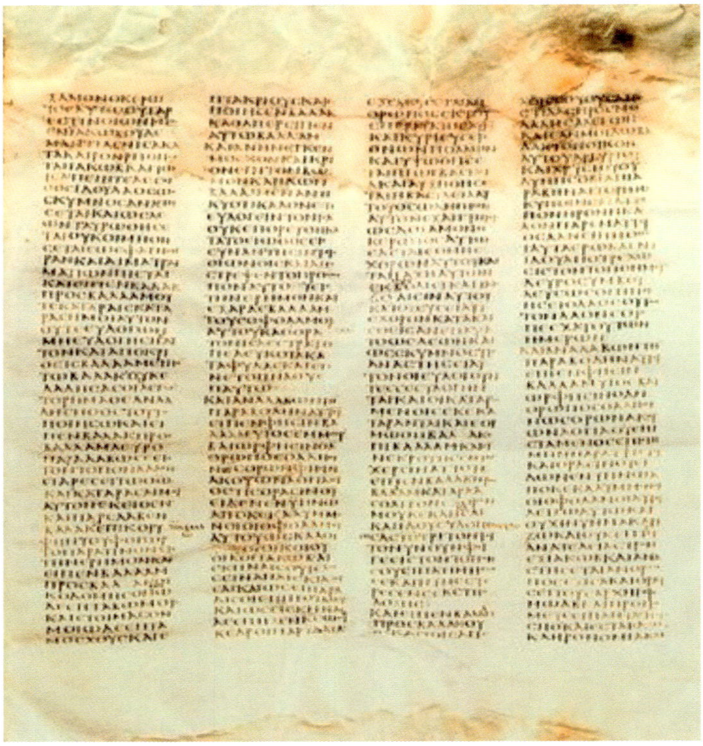

Page from the codex sinaiticus [8]

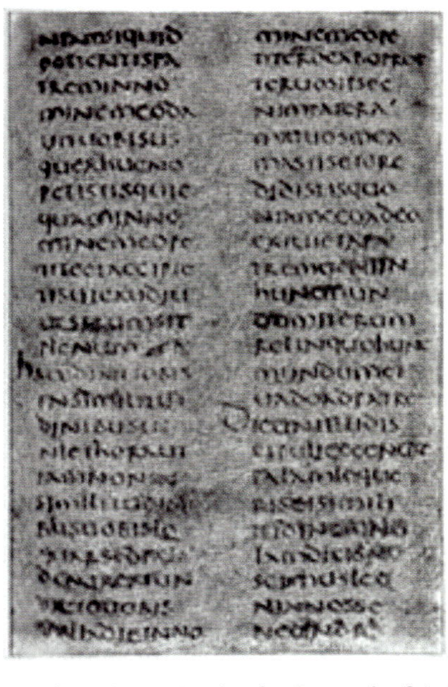

[9]

Verses from the Vetus Latina's **Gospel of John** 6:23–30

Written in ancient Latin the Vetus Latina is a collection of Latin translations of biblical texts from the Old and New Testaments which are dated from around AD 350.[10]

In AD 382 the use of the Greek language in Rome was declining and Latin became the common language. So that the people could understand the scriptures Pope Damasus commissioned St Jerome to revise the Latin versions of the Gospels which were in circulation at that time. This version of the bible became known as the Vulgate, which eventually became the generally accepted version of the Bible.[11]

St Jerome AD 347—420 [12]

Jerome's translation was not immediately accepted, but from the mid 6th century a complete Bible with all the separate books bound in a single cover was commonly used. It usually contained Jerome's Old Testament translation from Hebrew, and his revision of the Greek Gospels.[13] It is extracts from the Vulgate which are written in the Book of Deer.

THE ORIGINAL BOOK OF DEER

The Cambridge University report dates The Book of Deer as being written AD 850 – 1000. The writing materials are parchment of vellum made from animal skin, a quill pen and oak gall ink. The text is written in Latin, but in an Insular script, a medieval script invented in Ireland.

It is described as a "small volume, in parchment, of over eighty folios.[14] It is thought that the manuscript was written by one scribe and the bulk of the contents consists of the gospels of the four apostles. There is no doubt that it would have been copied from a similar document. Evidence plainly shows that the scribe was not familiar with the language he was copying by the numerous spelling and grammatical mistakes and misinterpretations made. The location where the extracts from the Bible were written in unknown as is the scribe. The Latin used is close to that written in the Vulgate Bible, or similar to the Irish Gospel text which had not been used in Rome for many years.[15]

The Book of Deer is copiously illustrated throughout with a collection of full page drawings, each of which is enclosed in an intricate border. There are four drawings of a main character, full pages with several characters and a half page illustration at the end of John's Gospel. The book finishes with two full page illustrations. There is also an assortment of marginalia or scribbles, doodles or illuminations at various locations throughout.[16] The text on the first page of each Gospel is also enclosed in a border and begins with an illuminated initial.

The manuscript contains the first six chapters of St Matthew's Gospel, and the first to the twenty-second verse of the seventh chapter; the first four chapters of St Mark's and the first to the thirty-fifth verse of chapter five; the first three chapters of St Luke's and the first verse of the fourth; with the whole of St John's.[17]

THE ILLUMINATION WITHIN THE MANUSCRIPT

The artwork is thought to have been carried out by at least two monks and perhaps a third.[18] The illustrations as identified by the Cambridge report are presented in order. The report also states: "Ornamental and minor initials: initials (2-5 lines) formed of black interlocking stripes, with geometric infill, tinted in yellow and orange, and human and animal heads projecting from finials, (located) at beginning of Gospels and Creed (2, 5, 17, 30, 42); versals (also) tinted in yellow and orange". Versals are defined as "Initials which are embellished".[19] The colours used would have been made from natural (vegetable or mineral) dyes.

Originally it was assumed that the portraits at the beginning of each Gospel were depictions of the authors, Matthew, Mark, Luke and John, but in recent times the identities of the characters have been the cause of some doubt. Amongst scholars there is no agreement regarding who the subjects in the drawings are. Indeed, they may be representations of holy men rather than portraits of Saints or prophets. In the report various suggestions have been made by renowned authors on the subject.

The report cites the following interpretations made by scholars:

> **Henderson**'s suggestion (Henderson 1986), is as follows:
> 4v, Abraham
> 29v, Zacharias
> 41v, Christ
> 85v, Ascension.

Geddes suggests (Geddes 1998) is:
1v, Two Evangelists and two other figures
4v, Matthew
29v, Zacharias and Luke 'compressed'
41v, Christ
85v, Empty cross
86, Four Evangelists

Marner's interpretation (Marner 2002) is:
4v, Christ (as warrior and Judge)
16v Healer
29v, Crucifixion
41v, Resurrected Christ surrounded by angels.[20]

It is interesting to note that these illuminations are all made on the back of the leaf.

The illuminated pages in order as they appear.

Folio 1v - Four figures, lower two with satchels, arranged around cross with star/flower in circle at intersection.

A remarkable similarity between the illustration on the page and the carving on one face of the cross-slab Pictish stone at Elgin has been noted. It has been suggested that the upper two figures represent angels, while the lower figures are evangelists carrying their satchels or shrines. This first page is similar in form to the illustration on folio 85v at the end of the manuscript.[21]

ELGIN CATHEDRAL CROSS SLAB

The Elgin Cathedral stone is a Class II Pictish Symbol stone/cross-slab with very fine, early Christian Pictish symbols on one face and a cross with interlaced pattern on the other. The stone was found in 1823 during repairs being carried out at Elgin High Street, within the former churchyard of St Giles. It was subsequently relocated to the west end of Elgin Cathedral Quire, on its north side. The front of the stone is divided into two panels, the upper having a cross with small hollows between the arms covered with zoomorphic interlace.[22]

Geddes states that "the stone is said to date from the 8th century and has been carved from a granite slab. There is no doubt that it would have been old enough to have been viewed by the illustrator (of the Book of Deer). In addition, the four intertwined animals depicted within a heart shape is reminiscent of the pattern used for some of the ornamented initial letters within the manuscript".[24]

23

Cross-slab at Elgin, Moray

Folio 4v - Facing the start of Matthew's Gospel. Bearded, seated figure (head partially effaced by staining) holding a sword and flanked by two small figures.

On close inspection of the artistic work of folio 4v it is not improbable that this illustration was made by a different and more accomplished artist than the images of all the others. The figure is more detailed and generally less rounded than the more primitive style used for the other subjects. Regarding the detail Geddes notes "the four-pointed beard and the folds of the drapery have been debated as well as the use of a sword in the illustration".[25]

Folio 16v - Facing the start of Mark's Gospel. Figure with halo and satchel.

Folio 29v - Facing the start of Luke's Gospel. Figure with halo and satchel, his hands reaching out through frame.

Folio 41v - Facing the start of John's Gospel. Figure with satchel, flanked by six small figures.

Interpretation of the six miniatures vary in the same way as the identity of the full-size subjects.

Folio 84v - Two figures with satchels at the end of St John's Gospel.

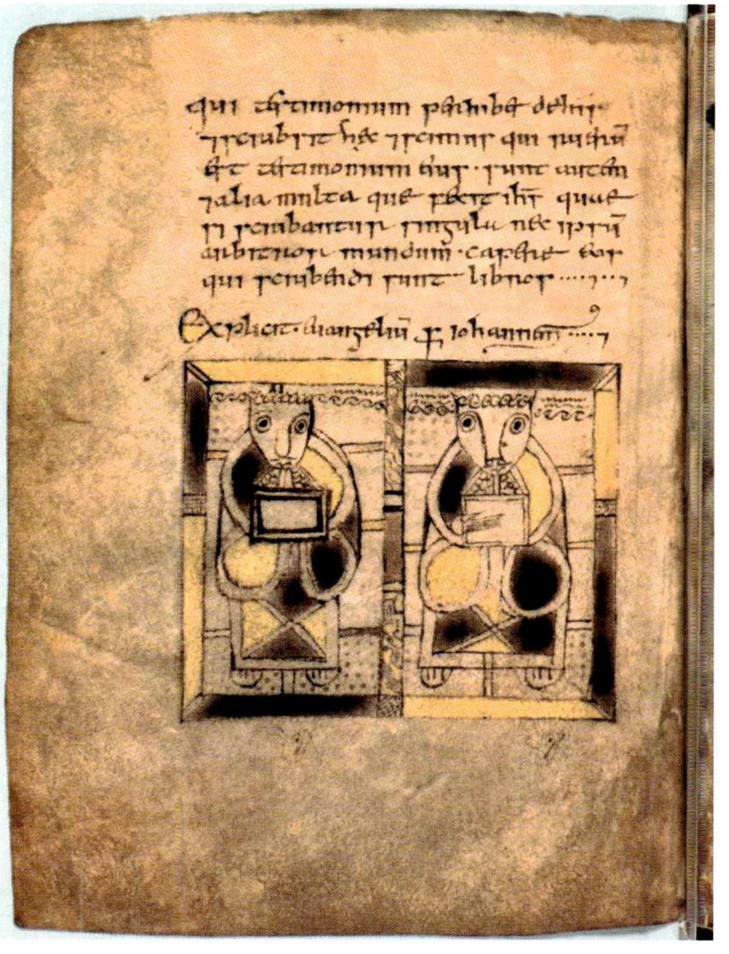

Having studied the drawing for some time two comments are offered:

First – the eyes of the figures at the beginning of the Gospels of both Matthew and John are almond shaped, in contrast to the eyes of all other human subjects which are rounded. This may indicate the work of a different artist.

Second – the use of circles in both the portraits and other illustrations is quite marked even if some are more defined than others. The halo-like symbol may be of some significance.

There is also some debate regarding whether the objects the evangelists carry at the front of their chest is a satchel or a house-shaped shrine. Most scholars have generally accepted that the object was a satchel used to carry a Gospel book such as the Book of Deer. However, the question is "Why would a satchel be carried at the front rather than at the side?" On closer examination it is evident that the object is house shaped. An example of such an object is the 8th century Monymusk reliquary. According to the National Museum of Scotland, *"Reliquaries housed precious relics associated with Christian saints, although the Monymusk Reliquary is now empty".*

26

Monymusk Reliquary

It must be asked – why would an evangelist, preacher or monk carry such an object around with them? Another possible explanation for the use of such an object is proposed: Could such a container hold the requirements for religious ceremonies?

Indeed, a Gospel book may have been one object in the casket, but it may have been used to convey other items such as a bowl or spoon, examples of which were found in Shetland amongst the St Ninian's Isle Treasure. A container with holy oil may also have been included.

27

Part of the St Ninian's Isle Treasure

28

This is an example of a chasse or casket:

Box with angels, intended to contain small bottles of holy oils. Early 13th Century. By Unknown (Limoges, France)

29

This is a photograph of a casket containing the three holy oils used during the religious rite of visitation of the sick, baptism and the eucharist.

THE APOSTLES' CREED

Returning to the 9th or 10th century Gospel book - located at the end of the book, immediately above the colophon, or final entry by the scribe and written in Latin at the same time as the Gospels, is the Apostles' Creed. The Apostles' Creed was based on Christian theological understanding of the Canonical Gospel, the letters of the New Testament and to a lesser extent the Old Testament. Its basis appears to be the old Roman Creed known also as the Old Roman Symbol. The Old Roman Creed, is an earlier and shorter version of the Apostles' Creed. It was based on the 2nd century Rules of Faith and the interrogatory declaration of faith for those receiving Baptism.

The Latin text of Tyrannius Rufinus: AD 344/5 – 411, (The Apostles' Creed)

> Credo in deum patrem omnipotentem;
> et in Christum Iesum filium eius unicum, dominum nostrum,
> qui natus est de Spiritu sancto ex Maria virgine,
> qui sub Pontio Pilato crucifixus est et sepultus,
> tertia die resurrexit a mortuis,
> ascendit in caelos,
> sedet ad dexteram patris, unde venturus est iudicare vivos et mortuos;
> et in Spiritum sanctum,
> sanctam ecclesiam,
> remissionem peccatorum,
> carnis resurrectionem.
>
> I believe in God the Father almighty;
> and in Christ Jesus His only Son, our Lord,
> Who was born of the Holy Spirit and the Virgin Mary,
> Who under Pontius Pilate was crucified and buried,
> on the third day rose again from the dead,
> ascended to heaven,
> sits at the right hand of the Father,
> whence He will come to judge the living and the dead;
> and in the Holy Spirit,
> the holy Church,
> the remission of sins,
> the resurrection of the flesh (the life everlasting)[30]

Folio 85r - The Apostles' Creed.

THE COLOPHON OR PLEA

From the 6th century onward it was not unusual to find the scribe had added a colophon or statement which provided facts such as his name and the date and place of his completion of the work, sometimes accompanied by an expression of pious thanks for the end of his task.[31]

At the end of the Book of Deer the scribe adds his colophon written in his own native language – Scot's Gaelic.

Forchubus catchduini imbia arrath inlenbran colli aratardda bendacht foranmain intruagain rodscribi....

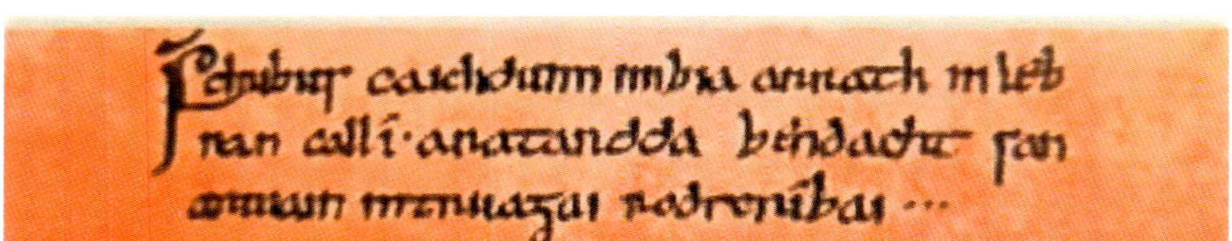 [32]

The Colophon

Stuart translated this as:

"(Be it) on (the) conscience of every-one in whom shall be for grace the booklet with splendour: that he give a blessing on (the) soul of the wretchock who wrote it".[33]

A less formal translation reads:

> *"Let it be on the conscience of everyone who uses this splendid little book, that they say a blessing for the soul of the wretch who wrote it."* [34]

Although this final statement invokes a degree of pathos it also seems to convey a sense of pride in his workmanship, as indeed he had every right to do so!

Importantly, this is the first written evidence of Gaelic writing surviving in Scotland.

THE FINAL ILLUMINATIONS

The final two pages of the book consists of full-page illustrations of four figures arranged around a cross with a circle at the intersection: the first showing three of the figures with their hands outstretched into the frame; the second includes two figures in lower compartments with satchels.

As ever, the meaning attached to the illustrations is unclear. It has been suggested that the empty cross signifies the risen Lord and the final page is either related to the ascent to heaven, or to the Revelations of St John.[35]

Wooden carving of the page before St John's Gospel courtesy of

Sandy Ritchie

with kind permission

Folio 85v

Folio 86r

MARGINALIA IN THE ORIGINAL BOOK

BORDERS

The most iconic examples of Insular art can be found in the illuminated manuscripts produced in the British Isles from the 5th to the 8th centuries. Illuminated manuscripts were most prevalent in religious writings and almost exclusive to the clergy and the upper class. These documents were typically produced by the monks at the Christian monasteries. By the 7th century the Medieval books were often decorated with ornate borders and letters. This is true of the Book of Deer. One of its distinctive features is the interlace decoration used to frame the borders on some of the full-page illustrations. These borders are filled with intricate patterns. Circles and crosses are amongst the other geometric motifs which may further embellish the art.[36]

The artist illuminates the borders with patterns which range from Celtic Key patterns which are based on straight lines and arrowheads as well as the loosely and flowing Celtic knotwork. Some of the border patterns are found on Pictish stones:

37

St Fergus church, Dyce Cross-slab

38

Rodney's stone, Brodie Castle. Displays both key and knotwork

ILLUMINATED INITIALS

An illuminated initial is an enlarged and decorated capital letter, the first letter of a section of text. The space for these letters to be drawn would have been marked out and left blank while the scribe worked on the text. Initials were added after the text had been copied, perhaps by another scribe. Initials could vary from the basic pen-and -ink drawn letter to the most elaborate of letters. The main purpose of the letter was to provide a visual point of reference. Illuminated initials can look quite different even within the same manuscript. They also provide a visual point of reference, marking the division of the text into books, chapters, paragraphs and sometimes even verses.[39]

Within the Book of Deer there are four large decorative initials, three of which are comparable, in that the outline frameworks are generally similar in character and there are diagonal designs within the framework, two being encased with dots. All four have several animal heads incorporated within the designs.

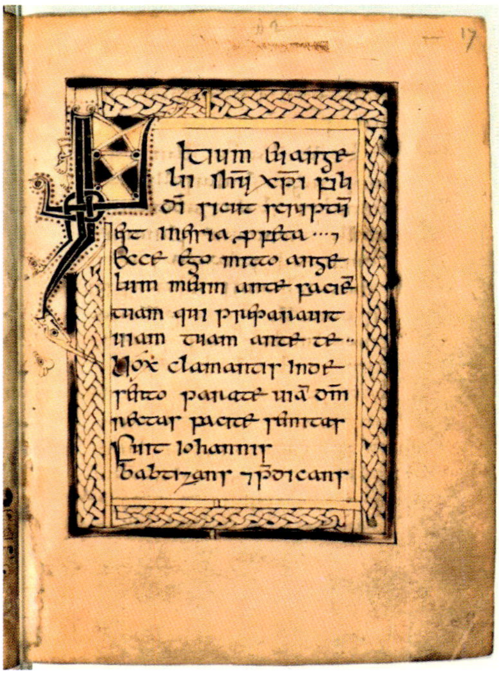

Folio 17r - Start of the Gospel of St Mark

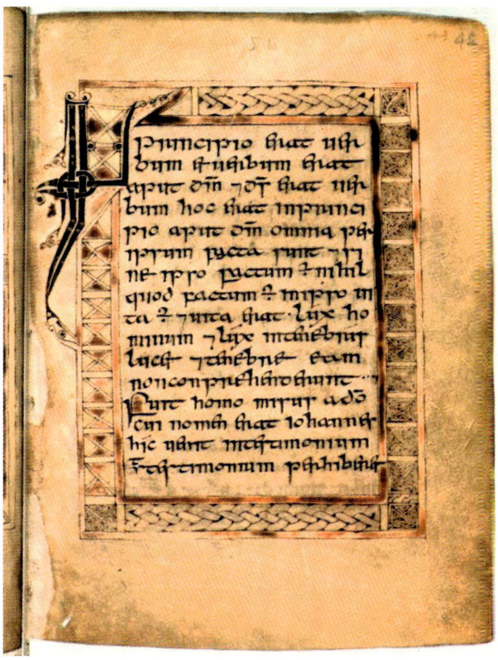

Folio 42r - Start of the Gospel of St John

The Chi-rho, the ancient Roman symbol representing the moment of the Incarnation of Christ, is created from the first two letters of the Greek name for Christ, Chi (X) and rho (P). It is formed by placing the rho so that it vertically intersects the downward stroke of Chi.[40]

Chi Rho pages in Insular Gospel books are generally located at the beginning of Matthew 1:18 and at the end of his account of the genealogy of Christ. It was usually marked with a heavily decorated page, where the letters of the firstword "Christi" are abbreviated and written in Greek as "XPI", and often almost submerged by decoration. The letters are written one after the other and the "X" and "P" not combined in a monogram.[42] This is so in the Book of Deer. As well as the numerous animal heads incorporated in the decoration, of particular interest is the figure of a human head located at the top of the initial.

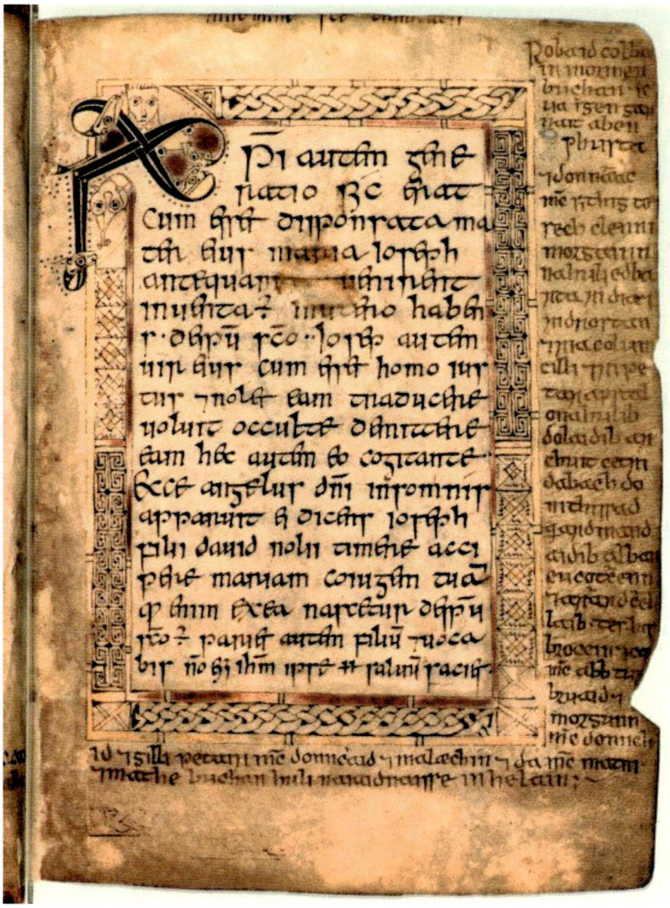

Folio 5r -

Chi Rho symbol of St Matthew's Gospel

“DOODLES” AND THEIR SIGNIFICANCE

As well as the text and the illuminations the book contains several drawings or “doodles”. These are mainly located in the Gospel of St John. The Cambridge University report states: There are - “numerous drawings of animals, birds, human figures or simple fan-like shapes in black ink, some tinted in (*colours which today appear to be*) yellow and orange. (e.g., 41v, 44, 45v, 51v, 54v, 67, 71v)”. It is suggested that these marginalia are the result of the artist trying out the new nib of his quill and are no more than doodles.[43] However, it is also claimed that the particular subjects drawn are strategically placed in order to emphasise the importance of a particular statement in the Gospels. The bird being cited at the text relating to the Eucharist and the figure of a man at prayer is related to the coming of the Holy Spirit. While other creatures may be a sign that point to a specific portion of the text. It is suggested that the circular brooch-like drawing has a similarity to the lower portion of the Elgin cross-slab previously mentioned.[44]

In his “*Book of Deer*” Stuart illustrates a number and variety of the “doodles”. The four-legged animals and the heads with flourishes are undefined and are generally described as “beasts”.[45] However they may be of greater significance. The local Mormaer of Cé at that time was potentially a member of the Clann Cannan, also known as the Clann of the Dog or Waterdog (otter).[46] As the ruler of the province, he would also have been a patron of the monastery.

It is worth considering the possibility that the “doodles” may be more than idle scribbles, or even carried out while the scribe was considering his next challenge. These apparent scribbles could have greater significance.

It is suggested that the animal heads with squiggles for bodies are, in fact drawings depicting otters () swimming in a river with the heads above water and the wake made as it swims along. There may also be a more meaningful association between the otters and the hounds or dogs.

The significance being that perhaps the Book of Deer was not constantly handled and carried around by monks while they preached, but it was an item commissioned specifically for personal use by the clan chief or mormaer at the time. This may account for the book’s remarkable state of preservation.

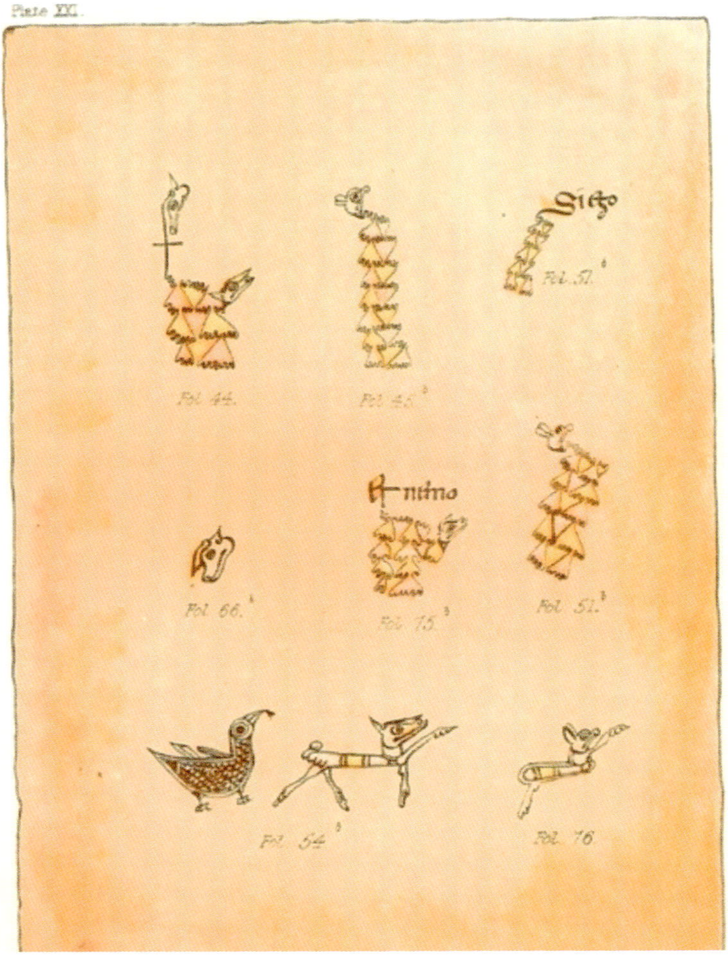

47

48

Yet again, it is possible some figures may be representations of deer, reflecting an association with the Monastery of Deer.

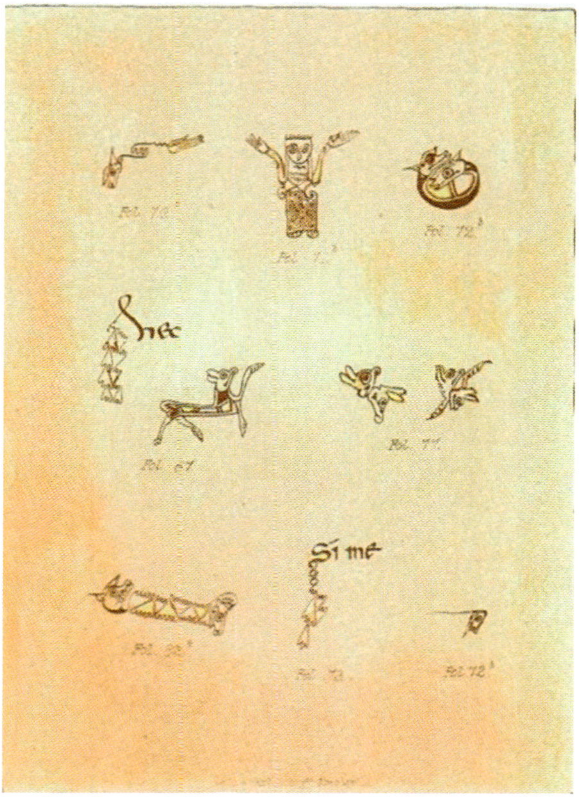

[49]

Interestingly, these drawings are also contemporary with some of the items which were discovered buried in a churchyard in St Ninian's Isle, Shetland. The "St Ninian's Isle Treasure" was discovered under a cross-marked slab in the floor of the early St Ninian's Church, on 4 July 1958 by a local schoolboy, Douglas Coutts. Coutts was helping visiting archaeologists led by Professor A. C. O'Dell of Aberdeen University at a dig on the isle. The silver bowls, jewellery and other pieces are believed to date from approx. AD 80.[50] The appearance of dogs and the numerous animal heads in the Book of Deer bear a remarkable resemblance to those depicted in the St Ninian's artefacts.

51

Scabbard Chape (The metal cover at the end of a sheath for a dagger.)

52

Terminals of a brooch

Another ancient treasure found locally in Deskford, Banffshire, is the Deskford carnyx, an ancient horn used in war and during ceremonial occasions. It may be contemporary with St Ninian's treasures being dated as somewhere between AD 80 and 200. It is said to have the appearance of the head of a boar.

[53]

Replica of the Deskford Carnyx

As for Pictish stones, the figures of beasts, be they deer, dogs, hounds, boars or mythical creatures, are depicted on the later stones by the sculptors. The horses and their riders are generally found in scenes illustrating hunting or warfare.

HERE IS THE END OF THE GOSPEL BOOK AS IT WAS ORIGINALLY WRITTEN

SOME TIME LATER AN IMPORTANT ADDITION WAS MADE

OFFICE FOR VISITATION OF THE SICK

The practice of anointing the sick developed from a Jewish tradition and was embraced by the Ephesians, followers of the teaching of the Apostle Paul. The record in the Book of Deer is the final part of the sacrament. The format is said to be influenced by the practice of the Eastern Orthodox Church.[54]

Instructions for the presentation of the ritual for the visitation of the sick are found in the Book of James in the Bible:

> *"Is anyone among you sick? Let him call for the elders of the church, and let them pray over him, anointing him with oil in the name of the Lord. 'And the prayer of faith will save the one who is sick, and the Lord will raise him up. And if he has committed sins, he will be forgiven."*[55]

The note of the portion of the *Office for the Visitation of the Sick* was added to the Book of Deer on two blank pages between the Gospels of Mark and Luke (folios 28v and 29r). Two reasons are proposed for this choice of location. Firstly that the monk did not have to turn the page when giving the rite.[56] But it has also been observed that the location of the Office is deliberately placed since it follows immediately after Mark's Gospel which ends with the healing of a woman with an ailment and the resurrection of a child who had died.[57]

Whether the visitation was written at the same time as the Gospels or added later is uncertain. The text is written in Latin by a hand other than that of the main scribe and the script has one sentence added in Scots Gaelic. Markus notes that David Dumville, who studies palaeography (old handwriting), proposes that it is likely to be almost contemporaneous with the original document, being written in late Celtic miniscule, with the addition of the instruction written in Old Gaelic.[58] Stuart states "It was added some time later".[59] Alternatively it is suggested that the visitation was added at or around the same time as the other additions. It is claimed by another authority to be "a 7th century prayer inserted into the book in the 12th century".[60] It appears that the argument provided by Dumville is likely to be the most accurate.

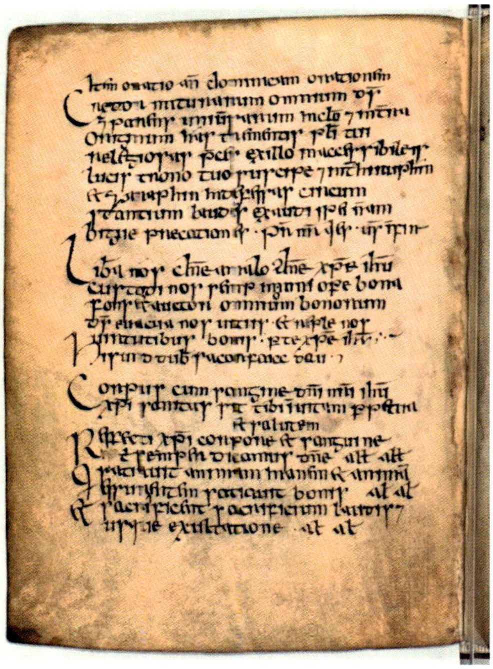

Folio 28v

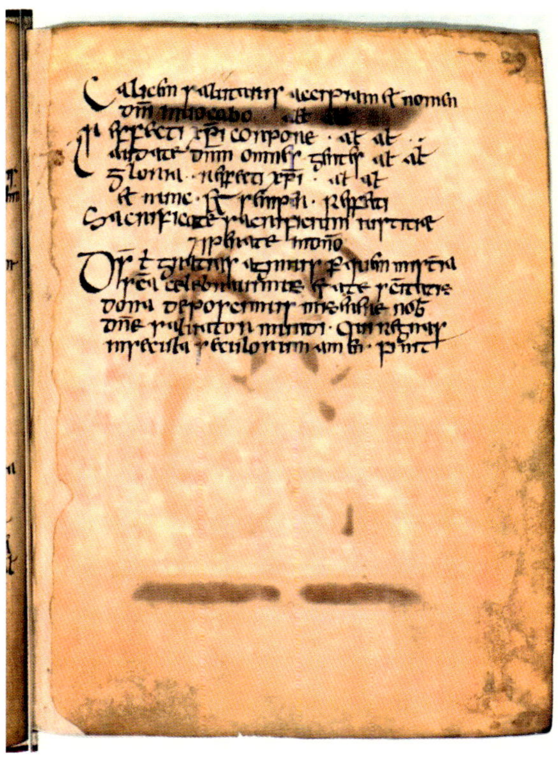

Folio 29r

The scribes Gaelic instruction is located on folio 28v reading "Hisund dubei sacorfaicc dau" translated as "Here give the sacrifice to him". This direction of when to give the sacrament is written in Gaelic at line fifteen of folio 28v. This is the second Gaelic entry in the book; however it may have been added some time later than the original entry of the visitation.

The cleric may chant most of the rite. The opening sentence is associated with what is known as the Mozarabic rite which is found in places where Christians lived under Muslim rule. It is known to have been in the Iberian Peninsula around the 5th century and it is supposed to have been used in Ireland sometime later.[61] The next portion of the rite is from the Vulgate Psalms 106:9 & 22 and 115:13. This is followed by a responsory statement taken from verse 1 of Psalm 116 which is repeated by the people present. Next comes Psalm 4:6 which invites trust in God and concludes with a prayer found in the Mass of the Gallican sacraments c. AD 700. The Gallican Rite was developed in Jerusalem and Antioch and translated into Latin in the 5th century. It is a version of Christian liturgy, used with other ritual practices in Western Christianity for the greater part of the 1st millennium and was thought to have been exported from Gaul to Ireland.[62]

THIS IS THE COMPLETION OF THE BIBLICAL TEXT

To many scholars the distinctiveness of the Book of Deer does not lie in the age or character of the Christian contents but in the fact that it contains the very earliest recorded writings of the Scot's Gaelic language.

Folio 45v. Doodle, possibly an otter.

From *This Splendid Little Book*— a Book of Deer Leaflet by the late A. Kellock with kind permission of his family.

4

The Book of Deer - The Later Entries

INTRODUCTION TO THE GAELIC ENTRIES

The Kingdom/Mormaerdom of Fortriu (Moray) in AD 1000 was dominated by the Ruadri and Macbeth families.[1] In Cé, modern day Buchan and Mar/r*, the members of Clann Cannan, the Clann of the Dog, or Waterdog (otter) and Clann Morgann, ancestors of the Clann Mackay, were the prominent families in the province. Cé, with its fortifications in the area of Bennachie during these times must not be ignored. Vikings invaded Scotland between AD 793 and 1266 and needless to say battles between various foes were fought, won and lost. It was a time when legends and facts were recorded and woven into the history of Scotland. In some way the later entries in the Book of Deer open us to the wider story of the emergence of today's country. During this period William the Conqueror invaded England in AD 1066 bringing with him many Norman barons whose influence gradually spread northwards. It was a short time later, between AD 1070 and 1093 that the leaders of the Celtic Church in Scotland adopted the rules of the Roman Catholic Church under the influence of the Queen, St. Margaret.[2]

There is no doubt that a study of the history of our country is fascinating, although here is not the best place for pursuing the development, especially since it diverts too much from the purpose of this book. The main points to highlight are the approximate dates of the first and final entries in the book and to examine the contents which were recorded within this timespan.

*Modern day Mar once was known as Marr which will be used here.

GAELIC ENTRIES

Around two hundred years after the Gospels were written, several other entries were added to the pages of the Book, some on blank pages while others were added around the written gospel texts. These entries are in Scots Gaelic except for the last one, King David's Charter, which is written in Latin. This is the first known substantial documentation using Scots Gaelic.[3]

The land grants were not all written into the book at the same time and may have been copied from original records. Some alterations were made by one monk to records made previously. It is suggested that the record of lands owned by the monastery, as well as other privileges, were inserted in the Gospel book in preparation for a legal petition to the king which would confirm ownership along with the right to be excused paying dues. This was eventually successful and resulted in the final entry, number VII, King David I's Charter.[4]

The entries may have been made over time as there were several scribes and different inks were used. There is no consensus regarding the number of scribes who made these notes. Authorities claim between two and six and Jackson says five and he names them Scribes A, B, C, D and E. It is Jackson's assertion used here. These seven entries are said to span the years from the latter half of the 11th to the mid 12th centuries.[5] During this time the rulers of Alba were: Malcolm III (AD 1057-93), Donald III (AD 1093-97), Edgar, (AD 1097-1107), Alexander I (AD 1107-24) and David I (AD 1124-53). Each king had sons and other close relations.[6]

ENTRY I – THE LEGEND OF THE FOUNDATION OF THE MONASTERY

The first entry is a legend relating specifically to Deer. It is this account of the foundation of the monastery, along with later writings which identifies the book as being in Deer at the time they were added. The scribe of the 11th or 12th century wrote the story as already described in Chapter 2 p. 20 & 21.

The legend starts on the tenth line of folio 3r beginning with the large letter C. It continues on the first eight lines of the following page, folio 3v. The author, or scribe A, immediately followed with entry II ending on the top margin of folio 4v. His writing starts small, gradually growing larger as he progresses.

The legend of the arrival of St. Columba and Drostan, his disciple, landing at Aberdour Bay and their request for land to build a monastery "is of a type familiar in the history of Celtic monastic literature, where it is standard procedure that the Celtic saint to whom the monastery or church is dedicated, who is reputed to have been its actual founder in the flesh, meets with the local lord, who may or may not be a heathen, and, by the performance of a miracle, persuades him to make a grant of land for the purpose. Commonly, the lord behaves in some aggressive manner to the saint, who miraculously humbles him; or, as in the present case, the saint cures him or some member of his family from a dangerous sickness, and in gratitude for this is given the land he asked for". The author continues "by inventing these 'foundation legends' the early monks, before the days of legal charters, provided their monastery at once with a remote 'historical' origin and a 'title deed'".[8] In the case of Deer, the first request for land was granted – it was the second request which was refused, followed by the son of the chief being cured of an illness by their prayers and thus gaining the land.

The lands granted:

Bede, Mormaer of Buchan gave to Columba and Drostan

Land from **Cloch in Tiprat** as far as **Cloch Peitte Meic-Garnait**.

Folio 3r

Folio 3v

It is in the Book of Deer that the offices of mormaer and toiseach are first recorded From various documents it becomes apparent that the Mormaer, or "Great Steward", is the senior kinsman of the dominant clan and ruled over the local population. Later he is the representative of the king. He governed a designated area of the kingdom of Pictland. As an owner of extensive lands he leased much of them to the residents in exchange for a rent and more importantly for the nation, he became responsible for providing the men, horses and armoury to fight for himself and later for the King in times of war.[9]

The toiseach is the "Administrative Assistant" to the mormaer, ensuring that his orders are carried out as well as acting as a judge in times of dispute. He too, has lands which he lets out for payment in kind and services as required. While the mormaer's position is hereditary, or at least kept within the clan, the toiseach, especially later, could be an appointee of the king. He was also responsible for providing hospitality whenever required.[10] The role of the Abbot, or later the Bishop, was as head of a Monastery. Religious centres were set up in Pictish nobles' estates so that each area of Northern Pictland, such as Buchan, had a monastery with an Abbot at its head. The Abbot played a political role in society as well as a religious one. The Celtic Church gave its blessing to rulers and gave God's authority to their leadership. In return kings and leaders granted land to the church to set up churches and monasteries in order to generate an income to support their practices.[11] The Abbot would have been a man of learning and probably a junior member of a noble family. It was his responsibility to ensure the laws of the church were obeyed and that any changes directed were implemented and maintained.[12]

THE GAELIC ENTRIES NO. II – VI.

These are the records of the land grants, written in native Gaelic by the scribes who used differing scripts and inks. It is these which makes the Book of Deer unique and firmly places it in the Buchan Monastery of Deer. There are five entries relating to gifts and favours, all differing in length. The scribes did not have blank spaces for their use, thus the records are spread amongst the pages. As well as sharing some space with the biblical text or an illustration one page has had a portion of text removed to accommodate the records.

Each identifies the donor and defines the exact lands granted to the monastery. They begin on folio 3v immediately after the legend of the foundation of the monastery (Entry I) and continue on the following three pages. They seem to be copies of records which may have come from an original source or sources. The donors are men of rank and status and the lands granted generally seem to be close to the probable location of the monastery of Deer itself. The period in which the grants were made is uncertain but some information about precisely who these donors were is included below each item. Unfortunately, the scarcity of contemporary records along with the unreliability of those which do exist, the different spelling of names and even the same person being known by more than one name, added to the vagueness of dates for events, has made certainty of information almost impossible. Sadly, the information relating to the mormaers and toiseachs of the Buchan area is particularly sparse. The dates of these entries are debatable although it is suggested that they are no earlier than AD 1058 but may be any time up to the mid 12th century.[13]

ENTRY II

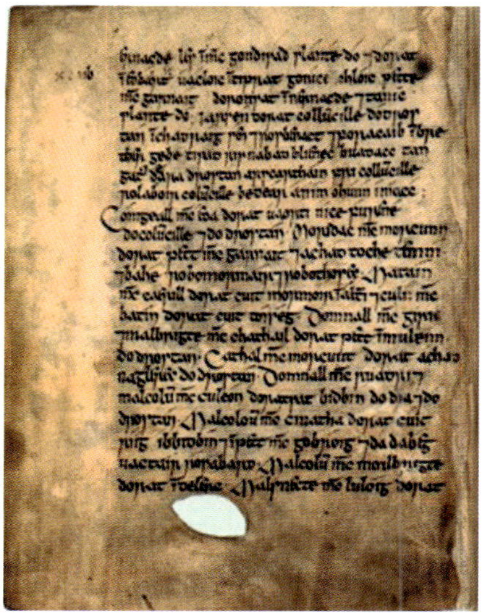

Folio 3v

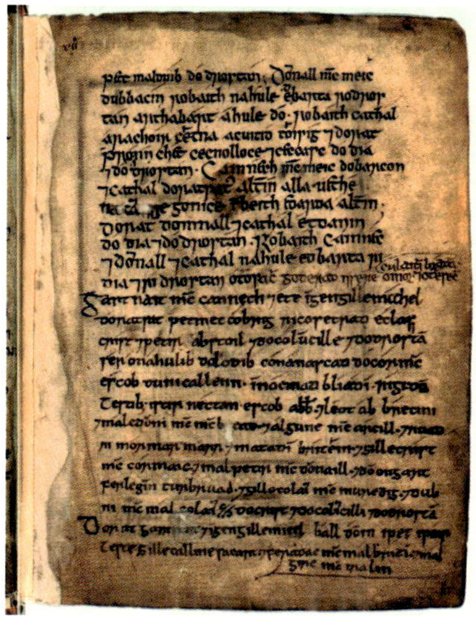

Folio 4r

Entry II starts on the ninth line of folio 3v with the large capital C for Comgell and continues on to folio 4r for the first 12 lines. The Entry is completed on the first two lines of Folio 4v.

Entry II is a substantial list of donors, lands and recipients which are listed consecutively by the same scribe who wrote the legend of Entry I. The list contains records of 14 separate donations. The lands may have been granted over a period even if the list was recorded simultaneously.

> *Comgell son of Aed gave from Oirte as far as Púiréne to Columba and to Drostán. Muiredach son of Morgann gave Pett Meic-Garnait and the field of Toiche Teimne; and it is he who was mormaer and was toísech. Matain son of Cairell gave a mormaer's dues in Altrie and Cú Lí son of Baíthín gave a toísech's dues. Domnall son of Giric and Mal-Brigte son of Cathal gave Pett in Muilinn to Drostán. Cathal son of Morgann gave Achad na Cléirech to Drostán. Domnall son of Ruaidrí and Mal-Coluim son of Cuilén gave*

Biffie to God and to Drostán. Mal-Coluim son of Cinaed gave a king's dues in Biffie and in Pett Meic-Gobraig, and two davochs of upper Ros abard. Mal-Coluim son of Mal-Brigte gave Elrick. Mal-Snechta son of Lulach gave Pett Malduib to Drostán. Domnall son of Mac-Dubaicín quenched all the grants in favour of Drostán in return for giving him his goodwill. Cathal quenched his toísech's dues on the same terms, and gave a banquet for a hundred every Christmas and Easter to God and to Drostán. Cainnech son of Mac-Dobarchon and Cathal gave Altrie of the cliff of the birch-tree of the river-bend(?) as far as the birch-tree between the two Altries. Domnall and Cathal gave Ednie to God and to Drostán. Cainnech and Domnall and Cathal quenched all the grants in favour of God and of Drostán from beginning to end, from mormaer and toísech till Doomsday. And the blessing of the Lord on every mormaer and every toísech who shall comply with it, and to their descendants after them.

The underlined italics was added at a later date by Scribe C, following the removal of the original wording.[14] It is interesting to note that he specially refers to the mormaer and the toiseach.

Most of what is known of those donors mentioned is from Woolf's "The Moray Question"[15] and Jackson's "Gaelic Notes".[16]

Comgell son of Aed - Mormaer.

Oirte as far as **Púiréne** to Columba and to Drostán. (Unknown)

Muiredach son of Morgann – Toiseach. Members of the Clann Morgann were one of the principal family groups in Buchan and beyond.

Pett Meic-Garnait and the field of **Toiche Teimne** (unidentified)

Matain son of Cairell – Mormaer, probably of Buchan.

gave a mormaer's dues in **Altrie.** Altrie is now known as Bruxie, and is included in the list of lands belonging to the Cistercian Abbey of Deer.

Cú Lí son of Baíthín - Toiseach

Toíseach's dues, presumably also of Altrie - as above.

Domnall son of Giric - Mormaer of Moray.[17] Giric may have been a senior bishop of the Moray region, he is thought to have been in post some time between AD 1093 and 1107.

And

Mal-Brigte son of Cathal – Toiseach of Moray.

Pett in Muilinn to Drostán. Estate of the mill. Possibly a mill on South Ugie Water.

Cathal son of Morgann – it is possible that Morgann, head of the Clann, had a son named Cathal who was the father of Mal-Brigte who, in turn, was also the father of MaelColuim (AD 1020 – 29), ruler of Moray. Cathal may have been a brother of Muiredach.

Achad na Cléirech to Drostán. "The field of the cleric".

Domnall son of Ruaidrí - while Ruaidri is the Mormaer of Marr. There is also the presence of senior members of the Clann Ruaidri in Moray.

And

Mal-Coluim son of Cuilén Tiasoch of Moray (possibly a brother of Constantine III, AD 995-997). These donors appear to have been descended from the rulers of Moray. It is proposed by Woolf that Kenneth son of Alpin (Kenneth McAlpin) had a son Aed (AD 876 – 8), who in turn had a son, Custanin (AD 900 – c. 943). He was the father of Illilb (AD 954 – 62) whose son Culen (AD 966 – 71) was the father of Custantin (AD 995 – 7). These are said to be members of the Clann Aeda meic Cinaeda. (Possibly Aeda son of Kenneth McAlpin).[18]

Biffie to God and to Drostán. Biffie is located south-west of Old Deer. It also belonged to the later Cistercian abbey.

Mal-Coluim son of Cinaed gave a king's dues (this identifies him as Malcolm II, AD 1005 -1034) Also descendants of Kenneth MacAlpin through his son Custantin (AD 862 – 76).

King's dues in **Biffie** and in **Pett Meic-Gobraig,** and two davochs of upper **Ros abard**.

A *davoch* is an area of land measure which has been described as "As much as four ploughs can till in a year".[19]

Mal-Coluim son of Mal-Brigte (probably the nephew and co-assassin of Findlaech, father of MacBeth, d. AD 1029). Woolf claims that these men are members of the Moray Clann Ruaidri. Jackson states he is "doubtless Mormaer of Moray". His brother was Gille Coemgáin.

Elrick. Elrick lies approximately four miles south-west of Old Deer. Elrick is also mentioned in the list of lands belonging to Deer Abbey.

Mal-Snechta (AD ?1058 -1085), Said to be King of Moray, son of Lulach. In AD 1078 he led resistance in Moray, but was defeated by Malcolm III (AD 1057-93), known as Malcolm Canmore. Lulach was the son of Gille Coemgáin Mormaer of Moray and his wife Grouch. Macbeth, the son of Findláech of Moray, was his cousin and is said to have been a grandson of Malcolm II. Macbeth became Mormaer of Moray in AD 1032 after he defeated Gille Coemgáin in battle. He subsequently married Gille Coemgáin's widow, Gruoch, mother of Lulach who briefly held the crown (AD 1057 – 8).

Pett Malduib to Drostán. Unknown.

In AD 1040, Duncan I, (AD 1034-1040), grandson of King Malcolm I, launched an attack into Moray and was killed in action by Macbeth's troops. Macbeth (AD 1005-1057) succeeded him as King of Alba in AD 1040. However, he was killed at the Battle of Lumphanan in AD 1057 by forces loyal to the future Malcolm III. Macbeth was initially succeeded by his stepson, Lulach, who was killed by Malcolm III, whose descendants would rule Scotland until the late 13th century.[20]

Domnall son of Mac-Dubaicín, Mormaer of Moray.[21]

quenched all the grants in favour of Drostán in return for giving him his goodwill. Here it appears to be a penance for a misdemeanour.

Cathal Toiseach of Moray.[22]

quenched his toísech's dues on the same terms and gave a banquet for a hundred every Christmas and Easter to God and to Drostán. This also may be an act of repentance.

Cainnech son of Mac-Dobarchon (son of the otter or water dog) Mormaer of Moray [23]

gave **Altrie** of the cliff of the birch-tree of the river-bend(?) as far as the birch-tree between the two **Altries.**

Domnall and **Cathal**

gave **Ednie** to God and to Drostán. Ednie is suggested to be in the parish of St. Fergus.[24]

Cainnech and Domnall and Cathal - these three may have been King, Mormaer and Toiseach or King and two Mormaers. It is also proposed that they may be brothers.

Quenched+ all the grants in favour of God and of Drostán from beginning to end.

+ Quenched - "Promised to protect."

Scribe A is said to have made these entries at a date later than AD 1058.
There are no witnesses to these records.

ENTRY III

Entry III continues immediately after Entry II on folio 4r and is written by Scribe D. Folio 4r is where the scribe removed the original text in order to record Entry III. The scribe's hand is said to be similar to, but not the same, as Scribe A's.

Folio 4r

Gartnait son of Cainnech and Ete daughter of Gille-Michéil gave Pett Meic-Gobraig for the consecration of a church of Christ and of Peter the apostle, and to Columba and Drostán, free of all imposts, with a bond for it to Cormac bishop of Dunkeld, the eighth year of the reign of David (1131-1132). These being the witnesses: Nechtan bishop of Aberdeen, and Léot abbot of Brechin, and Mal-Domnaig(?) son of Mac-Bethad, and Aluine son of Aircill, and Ruaidrí mormaer of Mar, and Mataidín the judge, and Gille-Críst son of Cormac, and Mal-Petair son of Domnall, and Domangart lector of Turriff, and Gille-Coluim son of Muiredach, and Duibne son of Mal-Coluim.*

***Imposts** – taxes or dues.

Gartnait son of Cainnech and Ete [his wife] daughter of Gille-Michéil (Earl of Fife).

Pett Meic-Gobraig for the consecration of a church. Mal-Coluim son of Cinaed, King Malcolm II, had previously given a king's dues from these lands.

Cormac bishop of Dunkeld. Succeeded by Gregory about AD 1135.

Known **Mormaers of Buchan** Cainnech (Early 12th Century), Gartnait (AD 1131) and Colbain (AD 1174), husband of Eva, daughter of Garnait.[25]

Witnesses:

Nechtan Bishop of Aberdeen, was the first Bishop of Aberdeen (AD 1125 to no later than 1150), after the seat of the bishopric had been moved to Aberdeen from Mortlach. The only contemporary sources for Bishop Nechtan are charters.[26]

Léot abbot of Brechin, is the first known Abbot of Brechin. He appears in two other documents: a letter from King David I of Scotland dated from AD 1150, granting the lands of "Nithbren" and "Balcristin" to Dunfermline Abbey where he is called "Alien abbate de Breichin". The other is a charter granted by King David to the church of St. Mar of Haddington dating from AD 1141 which mentions a "Leod of Brechin". He was almost certainly the father of the first known bishop of Brechin, Samson.[27]

Mal-Domnaig - son of Mac-Bethad (Macbeth).

Aluine son of Aircill, a witness to documents of the reign of David I and Malcolm IV.

Ruaidrí Mormaer of Marr (AD 1130's).

Mataidín the judge.

Gille-Críst son of Cormac.

Mal-Petair son of Domnall.

Domangart lector or chief professor of the monastic school at Turriff, sixteen miles west of Old Deer.

Gille-Coluim son of Muiredach.

Duibne son of Mal-Coluim.

This is the first of the entries to have a list of witnesses recorded.

ENTRY IV

This Entry is located at the bottom four lines of folio 4r. It is complicated by the fact that it is not written in sequence. The entry starts with a large letter and at the end of the line continues on the line above following a symbol possibly denoting the end of Entry III. It is completed in the bottom line and a half.

> *Gartnait and the daughter of Gille-Michéil gave Ball Domain in Pitfour to Christ and to Columba and to Drostán. Witness, Gille-Caillíne the priest, and Feradach son of Mal-Bricín, and Mal-Giric son of Tráillín.*

Gartnait and the daughter of Gille-Michéil (as above);

> **Ball Domain** in **Pitfour** to Christ and to Columba and to Drostán. Said to be "The deep spot", or hollow. Pitfour lies about a mile north-north-east of Old Deer.

Witnesses:

Gille-Cailline – the priest

Feradach, son of Mal-Bricin
Mal-Giric son of Tráillin

ENTRY V

On the top 2 lines of folio 4v is the completion of Entry II.

Entry V is written in the left margin and continues along the bottom of the page. This is mainly written by Scribe B except for the final two lines which were added later by Scribe C. Scribe C uses a lighter ink and adds a statement similar to that which he added at the end of Entry II. It is speculated that Scribe C was adding these statements in order to strengthen the claims they were about to make at the Moot Hill. Both these statements are underlined in the translations.

Folio 4v

Donnchad son of Mac-Bethad son of Ided gave Auchmachar to Christ and to Drostán and to Columba, in freedom till Doomsday. In witness of it, Mal-Fhéichín and Comgell and Gille-Críst son of Finguine, as testimony, and Mal-Coluim son of Moiléne. Cormac son of Cennéitech gave as far as Skillymarno. Comgell son of Cainnech, toísech of Clann Chanann, gave to Christ and to Drostán as far as the great pillar-stone at the end of the thicket nearest to Ailldin Ailenn, from Dubuice to Lurchaire, both rough-

grazing and pasture, <u>free of toisech till Doomsday; and his curse on everyone who shall come against it.</u>

Donnchad son of Mac-Bethad son of Ided

Gave **Auchmachar** to Christ and to Drostán and to Columba. Auchmachar, " the field of Madchar" is located two and a half miles west of Old Deer.

Witnesses:

Mal-Fhéichín- also a witness to Entry VI

Comgell

Gille-Críst son of Finguine

Mal-Coluim son of Moíléne.

Cormac son of Cennéitech

gave as far as **Skillymarno -** three miles north of Old Deer.

Comgell son of Cainnech, Toísech of Clann Chanann must be Toiseach of Buchan.

gave to Christ and to Drostán as far as the great pillar-stone at the end of the thicket nearest to *Ailldin Ailenn*, from *Dubuice* to *Lurchaire*, both rough-grazing and pasture, free of toiseach till Doomsday; a great pillar-stone may have been a Pictish standing stone. Aillden Ailenn has been proposed to be Aden.

ENTRY VI

The following entry was made by Scribe C. It begins immediately after entry V and starts at the top right margin of folio 5r and ends in the bottom margin of the page. He uses a paler ink and his writing is described as "rather spidery". This scribe made alterations/additions to the entries made by Scribes A and B.

Colbán, mormaer of Buchan, and Éva, daughter of Garnait his wedded wife, and Donnchad son of Síthech, toísech of Clann Morgainn, quenched all the grants from all imposts, in favour of God and of Drostán and of Columba and of Peter the apostle, in return for the dues on four davochs' worth of that which should devolve on the chief religious houses of Scotland in general and on its chief churches. These being the witnesses: Bróiccín, and Cormac abbot of Turriff, and Morgann son of Donnchad, and Gille-Petair son of Donnchad, and Mal-Fhéichín, and the two sons of Maitne, and all the good men of Buchan in witness of it, at Ellon.

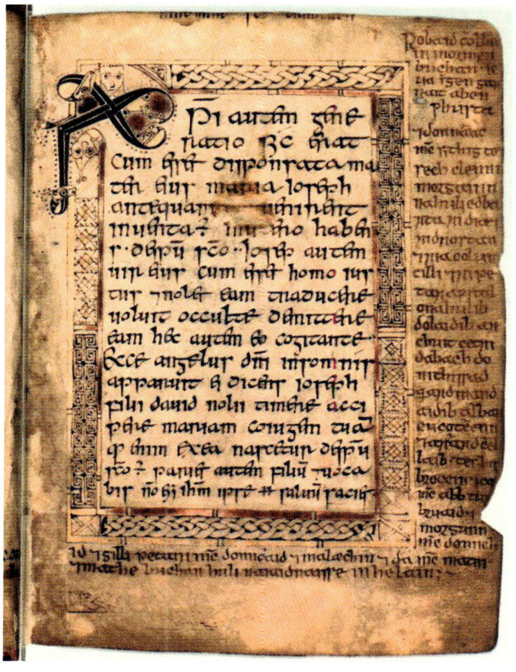

Folio 5r

Colbán, Mormaer of Buchan and his wife Ėva, daughter of Garnait, the previous Mormaer. Colbán took part in the attack on England in AD 1173 and was a witness to charters dated AD 1178-82. Between AD 1219 and 1233 he was named as "Earl Colbeyn".

And

Donnchad son of Sithech, Toiseach of Clann Morgainn.

quenched all the grants from all imposts, in favour of God and of Drostán and of Columba and of Peter the apostle, in return(exchange) for the dues on four davochs' worth of that which should devolve on the chief religious houses of Scotland.

It seems the monks were to pay taxes and dues on four davochs of their land, the proceeds to be given to the main church in Scotland.

Witnesses:

Bróiccín (The Judge) and Cormac, Abbot of Turriff were also signatories to King David's Charters between AD 1150 and 1173.

Morgann son of Donnchad and probably his brother, **Gille-Petair** son of Donnchad, perhaps sons of the Toiseach of Clann Morgainn.
Mal-Fhéichin
Two sons of Maitne. Gille-Aindrias, a witness to the Charter below may have been one of the sons.

It is suggested that Scribes A and B were contemporaries while C was later. Scribe D is no earlier than AD 1131.

Ellon - Nowadays a thriving town, the Moot Hill being the seat or meeting place of the rulers of Buchan and Mar where the court was held and justice dispensed. It is located close to the Ythan river and is commemorated by this memorial.

28

The Moot Hill Memorial at Ellon (Moot Hill c1100-c1795)

These are the total of entries made in the Book of Deer using Scots Gaelic :

- The colophon written by the scribe at the end of the gospels
- Instructions in the Visitation of the sick to "Here give the sacrifice to him".
- Entries 1 to VI

It is evident by the history of the entries and the amendments made to the earlier ones, which emphasis the roles of the mormaers and toiseach, that the monks felt they had been unfairly treated in being bound to pay imposts, either in money or in kind to their superiors.

ENTRY VII

KING DAVID'S CHARTER

King David I, youngest son of Malcolm III and Margaret and the third of their children to be King of Scotland, was for a time living at the English court of King Henry I and his wife Matilda, David's sister. He became familiar with the feudal system of laws and rules imposed by the Norman king. David I ruled from AD 1124 – 53. After arriving in Scotland he defeated his rival, the Mormaer of Moray, in battle and united the kingdom of Scotland. He then proceeded to introduce a feudal system of his own granting lands to a number of Norman nobles who had accompanied him from England.[30]

King David 1 from the Kelso Charter.

The final entry in the book of Deer is dated between AD 1140 and 1153, most likely 1150.[31] It is a copy of a deed written in Latin, granted to the monastery of Deer by King David I. In the Annals of Banff it is recorded that a similar Charter was [29] granted to the monks of Urquhart (Morayshire) by King David.[32] The Priory of Urquhart was founded in AD 1125 as a dependant of the Abbey of Dunfermline and was liberally endowed with lands, most of which were feued out to others. In AD 1345 Urquhart Priory was amalgamated with the Priory at Pluscarden and the buildings were left to decay and the stones used for other purposes. Its location is now marked by the Abbey Well.[33]

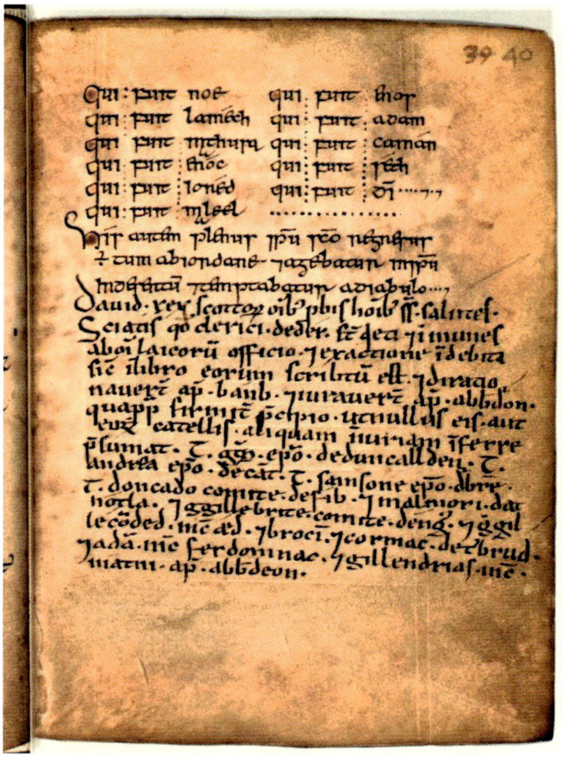

Folio 40r

This entry was made by Scribe E on folio 40r, nearer the end of the book. His hand is described as being Hiberno-Saxon with a continental influence, appropriate for royal charters.

King David's charter to the Monastery of Deer starts on the tenth line of folio 40r and reads:

> *"David king of Scots, to all his good men, greetings. You are to know that the clergy of Deer are to be quit and immune from all lay service and improper exaction, as is written in their book, as they proved by argument at Banff and swore at Aberdeen. Wherefore I strictly enjoin that no-one shall dare to do any harm to them or to their goods. Witness, Gregory bishop of Dunkeld. Witness, Andrew bishop of Caithness. Witness, Samson bishop of Brechin. Witness, Donnchad earl of Fife and Mal-Moire of Atholl*

and Gille-Brigte earl of Angus, and Gille-Coimded son of Aed, and Bróiccín, and Cormac of Turriff, and Adam son of Ferdomnach, and Gille-Aindrias son of Maitne; at Aberdeen."[34]

The information relating to the witnesses to the Charter is proposed to be :

Gregory Bishop of Dunkeld (d. AD 1169).

Gregory was bishop in the time of King David I. He was contemporary with Bishop Andrew of Caithness, Robert Abbot of Scone and Bryce Abbot of St. Colms.[35]

Andrew Bishop of Caithness

Andrew was bishop in the time of both David and Malcom IV (AD 1153 – 65) and was witness to a variety of royal documents. He was a contemporary of Richard, Bishop of St. Andrews and Samson Bishop of Brechin. He died in AD 1184 during the Reign of King Malcolm.[36]

Samson (Sampson), Bishop of Brechin (AD 1150 – 1165)

He is a witness to a charter of King Malcolm IV to St Andrews before AD 1158 and is a contemporary of Bishops; Matthew of Aberdeen, Andrew of Caithness and Simon and Richard of Moray.[37]

Donnchad Earl of Fife. (Duncan I, AD 1113-1154). Duncan was head of the native Scottish nobility. The Earls of Fife were the highest ranking nobles in the realm, and had the right to crown the King of Scots. As the premier Earl of Scotland he was the first to have his territory regranted to him by feudal charter by King David I in AD 1136.[38]

Mal-Moire Earl of Atholl

He was Mormaer of Atholl at the beginning of the 12th century, until sometime perhaps in the 1130s. According to the *Orkneyinga Saga*, Máel Muire was a son of King Donnchad and a younger brother of King Máel Coluim II. A Malmori d' Athótla is mentioned in a charter relating to a year after AD 1130. If the first part is true, and the second part refers to the same Máel Muire, then this Máel Muire lived for more than 90 years, between the death of King Donnchad I in AD 1040 and the 1130s. It seems likely that his paternal grandfather Críná was also Mormaer of Atholl. Máel Muire then probably inherited the mormaerdom in compensation for not inheriting the kingship.[39]

Gille-Brigte Earl of Angus

The Earl of Angus is one of the earliest attested Mormaers of Angus. He was possibly a descendant of Dubacan of Angus. Gille Brigte is recorded as a witness to a charter dating to AD 1150. He probably fathered both Ada and Gille Críst. He was dead by AD 1189, when his son Adam was the Mormaer.[40]

Gille-Coimded son of Aed. An **Aed** is mentioned as the father of Comgell in Entry I.

Broiccin is also mentioned along with Cormac Abbot of Turriff in the list of witnesses in the previous entry.

Cormac of Turriff Abbot of Turriff.

Adam son of Ferdomnach His name as a witness is not found elsewhere.

Gille-Aindrias son of Maitne.

There are several persons and signatories whose identity is unknown, or information is very sparse. It may be that the information presented here is inaccurate due to one person being mistaken for another. Further investigation may clarify the situation.

A number of interesting facts are contained within this charter. Firstly, the mention of clergy belonging to Deer is confirmation that a Celtic religious settlement was located at Deer. Further, that they had been subject to taxes and dues and other services despite the promises made in the previous entries. Also mentioned is the fact that King David I had seen the Book of Deer and was aware of the records of land grants. In addition, it is evident that the monks had been through a legal process in order to confirm their rightful ownership of them, having appeared at Banff prior to the charter being confirmed at Aberdeen. Finally, the king bestowed his protection upon them.[41]

It is evident that several people mentioned in the entries are unknown, although given the passage of time, it is remarkable that some are still identifiable. The same can be said about the lands which were granted to the monastery. Although the spelling may be different it is possible to find the location of a number of these areas today, even after 1,000 years.

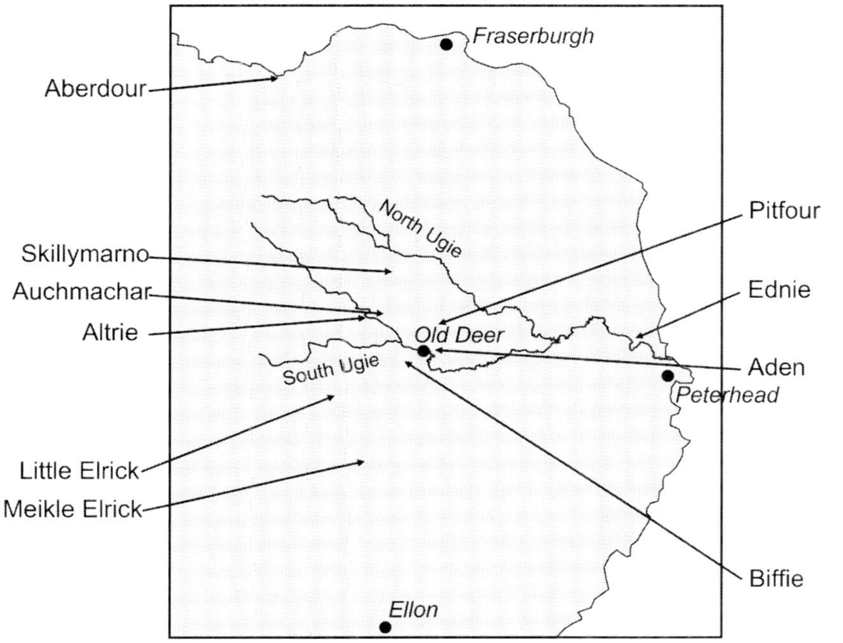

[42]

Map showing the locations of the generally acknowledged lands grantec

	The Gaelic names in the land grants
Aberdour from Entry I	Abbordoboir
Altrie (now Bruxie) from Entry II	Alteri
Biffie from Entry II	Bidbin
Little Elrick (north) and Meikle_Elrick (south) from Entry II	Elerc
Ednie from Entry II	Etdanin
Pitfour from Entry IV	Pet in Puir
Auchmachar from entry V	Acchad Madchor
Skillymarno from Entry V	Scáli Merlec
Aden from Entry V	Aldin Alenn [43]

Jackson is more reluctant than others to identify current locations. However, some additional sites have been proposed.

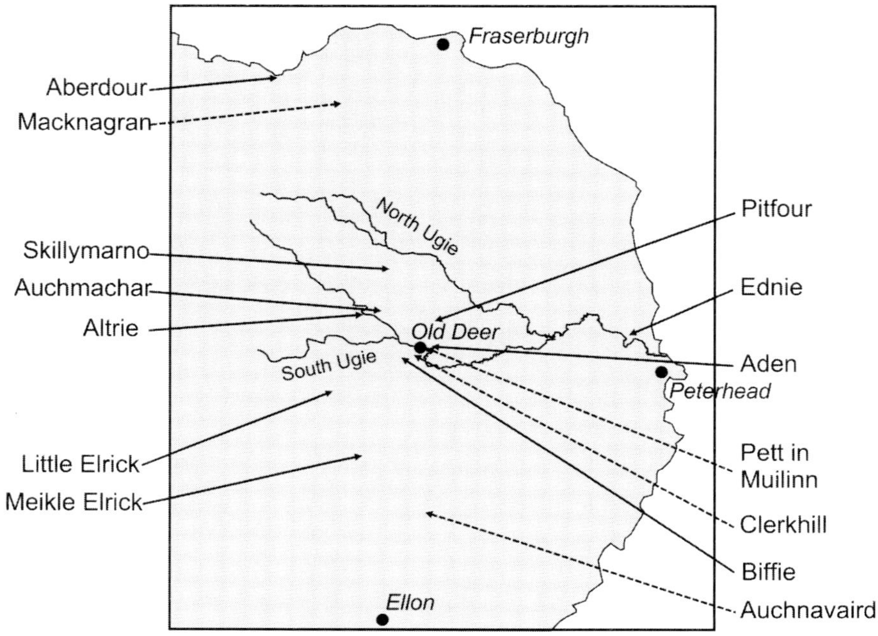

[44]

Map as above with addition of lands considered
to possibly be mentioned (the dotted lines)

Auchnavaird – from Entry II. Gaelic, Ros Abard – South of Meikle Elrick (Mains of Elrick).

Clerkhill – From Entry II. Gaelic, Achad na Clérec. The field of the Clerics – Wuddy Hill near Old Deer. Is this the location of the monastery?

Pett in Muilinn – from Entry II. Gaelic, Pett in Mulenn. The field with the mill – at Old Deer on the banks of the Ugie, now Mavisbank. It is speculated that the mill was a waulkmill, or a mill for fulling or finishing cloth. The process of fulling involved cleaning, thickening and stretching the woven cloth, especially cloth made from carded wool.[45]

Macknagran – from Entries I &II. Gaelic, Pette Mec Garnait. Derived from the lands belonging to "The son of Garnait".[46]

Some other possible names include:-

Auchentumb—from Entry II. Gaelic, achard Toiche Teimne. NW of Strichen.

Quithel— from Entry II. Gaelic, Achad na Clérec. An alternative interpretation to the above. West of Saplinbrae, Old Deer.

Cabra—from Entry II. Gaelic, Pett Mec-Gobroig. Lands of the son of Gobric (Cabra). Beside the White Cow Wood.[47]

The most interesting observation is the fact that the pattern of distribution, with few exceptions, is their proximity to each other. Could this be a clue to the location of the lost monastery?

Surely here is the proof, if proof were needed, that a settlement of monks was located around Old Deer and it is safe to assume it must have been a sizeable community if the lands it held are taken into consideration.

We are, however, left with the questions –

Where was it and can it be found?

LATER DEVELOPMENTS

Between AD 1120-1200, monasteries were a feature of the medieval world. Their increasing wealth contributed to lethargy and increasing spiritual weakness leading to a decline in religious commitment. The monks lost their monopoly of education as laymen became more literate while the use of monks as scribes became less relevant as printing evolved. Consequently, the influence of monasteries decreased while the authority of the king and the landowners increased. Thus, a shift in the power base took place. As to the Book of Deer itself, it disappeared for a number of years, only to be rediscovered by the Cambridge University Librarian, Mr Henry Bradshaw in AD 1860. It was part of the library of John Moore, Bishop of Ely. His library was bought by King George I who gifted it to the university in AD 1715. It is thought that Dr Gale, High Master of St. Paul's School, London, may have been an owner prior to that time.[48]

5

The Monastery of Turriff

THE PICTISH MONASTERY AT TURRIFF

"A monastery was not merely a place where prayers were wont to be said, and hymns chanted; it was a school of art, and industry, and learning, a centre of light and civilisation to the surrounding district." The author continues by describing the role of the Ferlengin as the monk "who wrote the books of the convent, and acted as the schoolmaster of the youth of the neighbourhood".[1] It is stated that, in addition to Iona during the time of Columba and his monks, there were fifty-three known monasteries in Scotland, many of them on islands. Celtic church rules were severe, resembling more those of the eastern church than the less strict rules of the western church.[2] A monastery required an open site, near but outwith a village.[3]

What is known of the Monastery at Turriff is only a little more than is available relating to the Monastery of Deer. In fact, if the monastery had not been mentioned in the Gaelic notes of lands granted to the monks of Deer, the existence of a settlement at Turriff may have long faded from memory. As with many reviews of records of old, the same information is repeated in various publications but cited from the same source. As with the Turriff monastery the authority on the subject seems to be John Stuart, Editor of *"The Book of Deer"* which was published by the Spalding Club in AD 1869.[4]

Apart from the notes of the land grants recorded in the Book of Deer most of the information is based on speculation. It is claimed that the history of Turriff is ancient. The site occupied by the monastery is described as "pleasantly situated on a broad table-land on the north side of the Water of Turriff (called Parcock in old charters) near its junction with the (river) Deveron".[5] The location is described as "a highly remarkable one, on the end of a promontory between two glens; the stretch of haughland below is known as Cruithen ruighe, the pasture land or cattle run of the Picts".[6] It was positioned at the brow of a lofty bank overlooking the valley of the Deveron, described as "a suitable site for one of those numerous monastic communities through which the knowledge of Christianity was imparted to the tribes of Pictland".[7] It was also said to be "one of the most important centres of the Celtic church betwixt Dee and Spey".[8]

Traditionally the monastery was founded by St. Comgan/Congan, an 8th century Irish priest, who is said to have left Ireland and founded Christian settlements in and around Lochalsh. He later moved eastwards and worked around Beauly and the Moray Firth for some time. He then moved to Aberdeenshire and settled in Turriff where he founded a monastery. Congan may have been the founder or it may have been dedicated in his name. It is said that "Congan, also known as Coan, Cowan, and Comgan, a Christian Prince mentioned in the Irish Martyologies, lived at the end of the 6th Century. Expelled from his home by non-Christian neighbours, he, his mother Kentigerna, and his nephew Fillin (or Fillan) went to the holy island of Iona, arriving there probably immediately after the time of St Columba. During his lifetime Congan voyaged from Iona about the coasts of the Highlands and Islands of Scotland where he established 13 chapels or churches and a 14th further away at Turriff in Aberdeenshire". The author continues "When he came to Aberdeenshire, Congan first established himself next to a major Pictish settlement at Balmellie Crofts at a place now known as St Congan's Den. Soon after arriving he built his church a mile further to the west, about which the town of Turriff grew".[9]

It is not impossible that monks visited each other to report new rules or discuss other church business. The Monks stone, found in Papil, Shetland, gives an illustration of what appears to be the abbot accompanied by monks on such a journey.

[10]

Papil - Monk's stone

"A trackway known as the Monks' Way, part of which still exists, led from Deer Abbey via Delgaty Castle and past Balmellie Crofts to the monastery. Importantly, two trackways from the coast of the Moray Firth to the settlements at Bennachie led past this settlement."[11] The monks of Deer may have travelled to Turriff by way of the riverbanks of the South Ugie, Idoch Water and the Burn of Turriff leading to the monastery at Turriff. In AD 1272, there was still a 'road of the monks' at Turriff.[12]

Bressay Stone
(Obverse)

Bressay Stone
(Reverse)

[13]

The Bressay Cullingsburgh stone shows monks on both faces dressed in similar garments, two carrying satchels on the left side. Bressay is an island located in Shetland immediately to the east of Lerwick. The stone is now kept in the National Museum of Scotland in Edinburgh.

The monastery is known to have existed at least up to the middle of the 12th century when Broiccin and Cormac were witnesses to King David's charter to the monks of

Deer. It is stated that "St Congan's Monastery long preserved its identity, and so late as AD 1132 we read (in the Book of Deer), of Domongart the ferlegin or learned man at Turriff, while a Cormac is mentioned about the same time as Abbot".[14]

Of the seven entries in the Book of Deer six are written in Scots Gaelic, five of which record grants of lands given to the monastery of Deer where the names of the witnesses are recorded, some from Turriff. The final entry is a copy of King David I's charter which is written in Latin. Two of the signatories to this charter are also described as being from Turriff.

GAELIC NOTES FROM THE BOOK OF DEER AND TRANSCRIPTIONS

Entry III

Entry III is witnessed by Domangart, lector of Turriff. The lector, or ferlengin was the second most important man in the monastery hierarchy with only the abbot as his superior.[15]

> *Gartnait son of Cainnech and Ete daughter of Gille-Michéil gave Pett Meic-Gobraig for the consecration of a church of Christ and of Peter the apostle, and to Columba and Drostán, free of all imposts, with a bond for it to Cormac bishop of Dunkeld, the eighth year of the reign of David. These being the witnesses: Nechtan bishop of Aberdeen, and Léot abbot of Brechin, and Mal-Domnaig(?) son of Mac-Bethad, and Aluine son of Aircill, and Ruaidrí mormaer of Mar, and Mataidín the judge, and Gille-Críst son of Cormac, and Mal-Petair son of Domnall, and Domangart lector of Turriff, and Gille-Coluim son of Muiredach, and Duibne son of Mal-Coluim.*[16]

The date this entry was made is recorded as the eighth year of the reign of King David, that date being around AD 1132.[17] As previously mentioned, Domangart is designated as the lector of Turriff. Among his other responsibilities it was the role of the lector to read the scriptures, write or transcribe books and record deeds for the monastery. He also acted as the schoolmaster for the youths of the community.[18] The presence of such a person indicates the importance of Turriff as a seat of learning.[19]

Entry VI

> *Colbán, mormaer of Buchan, and Éva, daughter of Garnait his wedded wife, and Donnchad son of Síthech, toísech of Clann Morgainn, quenched all the grants from all imposts, in favour of God and of Drostán and of Columba and of Peter the apostle, in return for the dues on four davochs'-worth of that which should devolve on the chief religious houses of Scotland in general and on its chief churches. These being the witnesses: Bróiccín, and Cormac abbot of Turriff, and Morgann son of Donnchad, and Gille-Petair son of Donnchad, and Mal-Fhéichín, and the two sons of Maitne, and all the good men of Buchan in witness of it, at Ellon.*[20]

Here mention is made of Broiccin and Cormac, the Abbott of Turriff. There is a record of a Broiccin, Judex (Judge) of the King, who is witness to an agreement between Henry, the Physician, King's Clerk, and Niall MacIvar dated from AD 1189 to 1195. However, they may well be two different persons. Little is known of Cormac, Abbot of Turriff.[21]

Entry VII

Entry VII is written by the scribe in Latin and is a Charter from King David I. Broiccin and Cormac are again recorded as being amongst the witnesses.

> *David king of Scots, to all his good men, greetings. You are to know that the clergy of Deer are to be quit and immune from all lay service and improper exaction, as is written in their book, as they proved by argument at Banff and swore at Aberdeen. Wherefore I strictly enjoin that no-one shall dare to do any harm to them or to their goods. Witness, Gregory bishop of Dunkeld. Witness, Andrew bishop of Caithness. Witness, Samson bishop of Brechin. Witness, Donnchad earl of Fife and Mal-Moire of Atholl and Gille-Brigte earl of Angus, and Gille-Coimded son of Aed, and*

Bróiccín, and Cormac of Turriff, and Adam son of Ferdomnach, and Gille-Aindrias son of Maitne; at Aberdeen.[22]

Colban, Mormaer of Buchan died around AD 1187 and he was succeeded by his son Roger.[23] It is claimed to be Roger who erected a church and parish and may have gifted lands to the Knights Templar at that time.[24] Fergus was the last of the mormaers and he was the father of Marjory who was to become the Countess of Buchan.

It is observed that "Unlike other Celtic religious houses in the north-east, the little community at Turriff seems to have been extinguished instead of being converted into an establishment of Roman Monks or Canons Regular, as occurred elsewhere (for example at Monymusk and Deer)".[25]

When King David I returned from England to take up the monarchy, he was accompanied by barons of Norman descent who were familiar with the concept of Feudalism which structured society into lords, vassals, knights and serfs. The lord paid homage to the king and in return for land he was obliged to provide military service as required. The vassal promised to fight for the lord at his command, whilst the lord agreed to protect the vassal from external forces.[26] Knights were granted lands from their lord in return for fighting for the lord or king and the serfs worked on the lands. The role of the Celtic church was diminished when their lands were given to the new feudal lords.[27] A new monastic system was introduced, and it is probable that the old Pictish monks were absorbed into the system, possibly as lay members.

It was during King David's reign that the role of bishop was introduced. Gradually the diocese was defined and parishes each had a church whose priest was ordained and answerable to the bishop. Thus, the power of the church was moderated with the role of the mormaer and toiseach being adapted to fit the system as earl and vassal.[28]

The Barons were granted lands by gift or by marriage.[29] William Comyn became Earl of Buchan via his second wife, Marjory, daughter of Fergus, the last mormaer who died before AD 1214.[30] Through these changes the barons took over the powers and the laws of the country and the rule and influence of the Pictish church waned as the hierarchy of the church was enforced with bishops at the head and the lower ranks subject to the rules which were imposed by the Pope or the king.[31] The lands which once belonged to the monasteries became the property of the earls who endowed the monastery with part of the income earned from them.

At the beginning of the 13th century William Comyn started to build the Cistercian Abbey at Deer. Deer Abbey was originally ruled by monks from Kinloss in Moray and the occupants of the old monastery probably became the lay brethren of the Abbey.[32] The fate of the monks of Turriff appears to have been similar in as much as they were demoted from their monastic positions within the new religious orders.

Unlike the monastery of Deer, which was replaced by a Cistercian Abbey endowed by the Norman Earl of Buchan, Turriff monastery had been replaced by a hospital or almshouse, around the time of King David I in AD 1153. By about AD 1179 Turriff was formally erected into a parish and a new church was built at that time on a site in Turriff which had once belonged to the monastery.[33]

A document dated AD 1273 states that Alexander Comyn, Earl of Buchan, has constructed an almshouse at Turriff for the welfare of the soul of Alexander King of Scotland and had dedicated it to St. Mary and St. Congan. It was to house one master, who was to be presented to the Bishop of Aberdeen, along with six chaplains who were to wear the habit of secular canons. They were to serve God and celebrate divine service within the church. The hospital was to house thirteen paupers chosen by the Earl from the poor husbandmen of Buchan. They were to be free of taxation, service or other dues to their king or lord. The residents had to obey the laws or forfeit any property they may possess. The founding charter, witnessed by King Alexander III also describes the extent of the lands granted to the hospital. The charter also stated that "the Earl will supply the hospital with two chalders of meal and three chalders of malt, from his constabulary, receiving half on Pentecost and half on Martinmas".[34] Exactly when the almshouse/hospital was built is unknown.

The then new St Congan's church, which was erected around the time of the hospital, is said to have been built at this site in the 12h Century and the income from the lands were gifted to Arbroath Abbey in the 13th Century by Marjory, Countess of Buchan. The exact date of the later church is unclear but it is thought to be mostly medieval with the later addition of a choir at the east while other alterations were made through time. By the late 18th century the building had gradually degenerated into the roofless ruin it is today.[35]

36

Built into the wall is an interesting feature which is believed to have been removed from the hospital.

A weathered sandstone block carved with ten heads has been inserted into the gable (it is thought to have derived from the lost Hospital of Turriff and be a memorial to the Earl and Countess of Buchan).[38]

37

Postscript

Then and Now

As to the Monastery of Deer, who knows where it is located? A number of archaeological digs, predominantly funded by the Book of Deer Project, have been carried out over recent years with the aim of finding its location. Initially it was thought the monastery might have been somewhere around the site of the ancient ruined church of Old Deer. However, after several attempts, during which some interesting finds were made, the aim was not achieved. The digs were then moved to a site adjacent to the ruined Abbey of Deer and there appeared to be evidence of a settlement of Picts at an appropriate date.

But the question must be asked – what evidence must be unearthed to satisfy the scholars that there was indeed a monastery at this site at the relevant time. Indeed, although there is some indication of a settlement, is it the monastery? Meanwhile, some clues as to its whereabouts seem worthy of further investigation.

Wooden carving of an imagined Pictish monastery

by Sandy Ritchie with kind permission

EPILOGUE

An epilogue is defined as "a section or speech at the end of a book or play that serves as a comment on or a conclusion to what has happened." Thus, I wish to add some personal reflections made during researching and writing this book.

Regarding the contents of the book, I would consider it a halt at a siding during a railway journey where there is time to take stock of the progress made so far rather than assuming this is the end of the line. This journey has been in some way a lone adventure and for me a massive personal learning experience. On reflection there are so many ways I have had to re-evaluate my opinions as my greater understanding of events has taken place.

My initial concept of the Picts as an aboriginal people, unsophisticated and coarse, has been drastically altered inasmuch as I now see them as a collection of knowledgeable tribes and artisans of the first degree. The legacy they have left us in the way of their standing stones and cross slabs is inordinately priceless beyond words. At the same time, I fear the uniqueness of this precious heritage is underestimated in the extreme. The skill and craftmanship needed to create such intricate and long enduring items is awesome to say the least. These people were no primitive tribe but a collection of clever, resourceful, and enterprising artists worthy of comparison with today's most celebrated sculptors and fine metal workers. Their heritage lives on long after later inventions have disappeared. However, even today these Pictish skills are generally unappreciated and unrecognised.

Yet in other ways it has made me particularly conscious of people's general lack of awareness regarding the historical importance to our country, even to the residents of our own locality, concerning the extremely significant place the Book of Deer has in our history. Anecdotally I have noted that within our own population knowledge and appreciation of even the presence of the book is sparce. Furthermore, recognition of the magnitude of the significance of the first known written record of Scots Gaelic appears almost totally unheard of.

As far as investigation into the conclusions of how Christianity came to the Buchan area is concerned, they were derived from what appeared to be a logical pathway with reference to currently known information. The dates which generally concur with other evidence presented is acceptable since the evidence itself is sparce. However, it is acknowledged that the dates cited would contribute more to speculation than to fact. Yet, there is no proof that the theory proposed is in any way inaccurate in comparison to any other proposal.

Another item of interest is the objects being carried at the front of the monks' chests as depicted in both the Book of Deer and on the carved stones. These are generally named as satchels by students of the period. In my opinion they are caskets such as the Monymusk reliquary and are intended to carry special oils used during sacred rituals.

The original body of the Book of Deer contains the four gospels with some later ecclesiastical additions, predominantly written in Latin. The objects of particular interest, frequently defined as "Doodles" and inserted at the time of writing, are the dog-like animals and the heads finished with flourishes. I suggest they have a more compelling meaning. The Mormaers of Cé during this era were from the Clann Morgann who were known as the "Clann of the Dog". The hounds drawn amongst the text along with the embellished dog heads or otters may be of greater significance. The state of preservation of the Book of Deer may also be a clue to its ownership. It is possible that the book was never intended to be carried around and handled by various monks but was made by scribes for the private use of a member of the Clann Morgann, even for the use of the Mormaer himself.

As for the Gaelic entries, it is the first one which may be controversial. This is the record of the Legend of the foundation of the monastery of Deer. It is generally accepted that Columba did not visit the Northern Picts. His centre of power being Iona, part of Dal Riada, where another language was spoken and another family ruled over it. Furthermore, the dates for Drostan and Columba show that Drostan was the elder of the two. No, if anyone arrived at New Aberdour shore with Drostan it was Colm. Noting that the tale was added during the 10th or 11th century or 400-500 years after the event, by which time Saint Columba was far more renowned of the evangelists, it may have been due to the age of the legend or a deliberate move to add the name of the better-known person. St Colm was a well-travelled missionary who may also have been known as St Colman, the founder of the Monastery at Portmahomack.

Looking to the future, it is hoped that, with the development and use of modern technology along with the guidance and support of expert archaeologists, evidence of the location of the Monastery of Deer can be uncovered. There is no doubt that finding evidence of a settlement would put the location on the map and greatly enhance the reputation of the Book of Deer. On a personal note it is said "To travel hopefully is a better thing than to arrive", after all, it is a most enjoyable journey!

Folio 54v - Bird Doodle

Stuart, J. (1869). *The Book of Deer.* Spalding Club : Aberdeen

BUCHAN'S OWN ILLUMINATED MANUSCRIPT

The Book of Deer is a mighty precious thing
It may have belonged to a Prince or a King
Maybe it was used by a rich man or read to the poor
Who knows it might have even been kept in Pitfour.

It's pages tell the stories of gospels and of saints
But an episode in Scotland's dark history it paints
Its one-time home in Buchan is undisputed
There is no doubt that in Deer it is deeply rooted

With a history of mystery we cannot tell
If St Drostan really landed alongside a well
Why, where and when exactly it was written
Is not known to this day but the author is smitten

Between the ancient pages is so vibrant a story
Of dark ages and the shift of the power and the glory
From tribal leaders of local sects and clans
To the development of Scotia as a county it spans

So I request all readers of this small oration
To say Hallelujah to the birth of our nation.

REFERENCES

Chapter 1 – The Picts and Deer

1 https://en.wikipedia.org/wiki/Caledonia 25.05.2019

2 **Burford A.** (2000). *What happened to the Caledonians?* IN Cowan E.J. & McDonald A. Alba: Celtic Scotland in the Medieval Era. Tuckwell Press : East Lothian. ISBN 1 86232 151 5

3 https//en.wikipedia.org/wiki/De_Situ_Albanie 25.05.2019

4 https://commons.wikimedia.org/wiki/File:Pictish_kingdoms.png https://creativecommons.org/licenses/by-sa/3.0/deed.en - CC BY-SA 3.0, Lordpeyre. 13.11.2021

5https://en.wikipedia.org/wiki/Ecclesiastical_History_of_the_English_People 13.11.2021

6 **Hudson, B.** (2014). *The Picts.* Wyllie Blackwell : Chichester. ISBN 978-1-118-60202-7

7 https://en.wikipedia.org/wiki/Battle_of_Mons_Graupius 27.05.2019

8 **Noble G. Evans N.** (2019). *The King in the North : The Pictish Realms of Fortriu and Ce.* Birlinn : Edinburgh. ISBN 978 1 78027 551 2

9 **Grant, A.C.** (2020). *The Legend of Cruithne and his Seven Sons*

https://www.academia.edu/42060328/The_Legend_of_Cruithne_and_his_Seven_Sons 21.11.2020

10 https://en.wikipedia.org/wiki/Hadrian%27s_Wall 22.11.2020

11 https://www.britannica.com/topic/Antonine-Wall 22.11.2020

12 https://en.wikipedia.org/wiki/End_of_Roman_rule_in_Britain 22.11.2020

13 https://en.wikipedia.org/wiki/D%C3%A1l_Riata 23.11.2020

14 http://www.whithorn.com/timeline/st-ninian 24.11.2020

15 **Simpson, W.D.** (1925). *The Origins of Christianity in Aberdeenshire.* Wyllie & Son : Aberdeen

16 **Duncan, A.A.M**. (1978). *Scotland : The Making of a Kingdom : The Edinburgh History of Scotland* Vol. I Oliver & Boyd : Edinburgh ISBN 0 05 003183

17 **Scott, A.B.** (1918). *The Pictish Nation : The People and its Church.* T.N. Foulis : London

https://archive.org/details/pictishnationits00scot/page/n8

18 **Simpson, W.D.** (1925). *The Origins of Christianity in Aberdeenshire.* Wyllie & Son : Aberdeen

19 https://en.wikipedia.org/wiki/Bridei 25.11.2020

20 **Wyness, J. Fenton** (1925). *Sketch Map of Aberdeenshire.* IN Simpson, W.D. *The Origins of Christianity in Aberdeenshire.* Wyllie & Son: Aberdeen

21 **Duncan, A.A.M**. (1978). *Scotland : The Making of a Kingdom : The Edinburgh History of Scotland* Vol. I Oliver & Boyd : Edinburgh ISBN 0 05 003183

22https://www.undiscoveredscotland.co.uk/usbiography/monarchs/kennethi.html 17.11.2021

23 https://www.thebritishacademy.ac.uk/documents/2083/pba167p349.pdf 11.11.2021 Sir John Ryhs Memorial Lecture 17.11.2021

24 **Allen, J.R. and Anderson, J.** (1903) *The Early Christian Monuments of Scotland.* Balgavies : Pinkfoot

25 **Noble, G., Goldberg. M. and Hamilton, D.** (2018). *The development of the Pictish symbol system: inscribing identity beyond the edges of Empire.* **Antiquity,** Volume 92, Issue 365 pp. 1329-1348 https://www.cambridge.org/core/journals/antiquity/article/development-of-the-pictish-symbol-system-inscribing-identity-beyond-the-edges-of-empire/4F09B9

26_https://commons.wikimedia.org/wiki/File:Pictish_Stone_distribution.jpg – https://creativecommons.org/licenses/by-sa/3.0/deed.en - CC BY-SA 3.0, David Lloyd 13.11.2021

27 **Stuart, J.** (1856). *Sculptured Stones of Scotland.* Spalding Club : Aberdeen

28 **Cruden, G.** (1795). *Parish of Deer.* IN Sinclair, J. (1791). The Statistical Account of Scotland. Vol.1. Edinburgh p469-483.

29 **Brown, L.J., Martin, A.K., Melville, M.W.** (2021). Map showing Stone Circle and Abbey of Deer

30 https://cudl.lib.cam.ac.uk/view/MS-II-00006-00032 25.05.2019

31 **Woolf, A.** (2007). *The New Edinburgh History of Scotland: From Pictland to Alba 789-1007.* Edinburgh University Press : Edinburgh. ISBN 978-0-7486-1234-5

32 https://en.wikipedia.org/wiki/Constantine_II_of_Scotland#cite_note-30_ 28.05.2019

33 https://commons.wikimedia.org/wiki/File:Early_Alpinid_kings.svg – https://creativecommons.org/in the public domain_Angusmclellan 13.11.2021

34 **Duncan, A.A.M**. (1978). *Scotland : The Making of a Kingdom : The Edinburgh History of Scotland* Vol. I Oliver & Boyd : Edinburgh ISBN 0 05 003183

35 **Woolf. A.** (2007). The New History of Scotland: *From Pictland and Alba 789 - 1070.* Edinburgh University Press. ISBN 978-0-7486-1234-5

36 **Duncan, A.A.M**. (1978). *Scotland : The Making of a Kingdom : The Edinburgh History of Scotland* Vol. I Oliver & Boyd : Edinburgh ISBN 0 05 003183

37 **Cowan, E.J. & McDonald, A.** (Ed.) (2000). *Alba : Celtic Scotland in the Medieval Era*. Tuckwell Press : East Lothian. ISBN 1 86232 151 5

38 https://en.wikipedia.org/wiki/Earl_of_Buchan 30.05.2019

39 **Duncan, A.A.M**. (1978). *Scotland : The Making of a Kingdom : The Edinburgh History of Scotland* Vol. I Oliver & Boyd : Edinburgh ISBN 0 05 003183

40 https://en.wikipedia.org/wiki/Saint_Margaret_of_Scotland 11.11.2021

41 https://aclerkofoxford.blogspot.com/2012/06/st-margaret-of-scotland.html By kind permission of Eleanor Parker 12.11.2021

42 **Duncan, A.A.M**. (1978). *Scotland : The Making of a Kingdom : The Edinburgh History of Scotland* Vol. I Oliver & Boyd : Edinburgh ISBN 0 05 003183

Chapter 2 – How Christianity Came to Buchan

1http://www.goodreads.com/quotes/807622-never-let-the-truth-get-in-the-way-of- 22.07.2021

2http://www.ancient-origins.net/ancient-places-europe/golden-age-christian-picts-evidence-religious-production-portmahomack-006264?page=0%2C 22.07.2019

3 **Simpson, W.D.** (1922). *A Forgotten Aberdeenshire Monastery.* Aberdeen University Press : Aberdeen

4 https://www.facebook.com/ThePictishArtsSociety/photos/a.249624471832262/1218549148273118/?type=3&theater 22.07.2019

5 http://www.eccentricbliss.com/tag/st-drostan 22.07.2019

6 **Jackson,K.** (1972). *The Gaelic Notes in the Book of Deer.* Cambridge University Press : Cambridge. ISBN 978 0 521 08464 1

7 **Simpson, W D.** (1954). *Dundarg Castle: a history of the site and a record of the excavations in 1950 and 1951*. Aberdeen University Studies : Aberdeen

8https://en.wikipedia.org/wiki/Scotland_during_the_Roman_Empire#cite_note-7earlie 23.07.2019

9 **Duncan, A.A.M.** (1978). *Scotland The making of the Kingdom :The Edinburgh History of Scotland Vol.1.* Oliver & Boyd : Edinburgh. ISBN 0 05 003183 X

10 **Scott, A.B. Rev.** (1917). *The Pictish Nation, its People and its Church*. T.N. Foulis : Edinburgh

11 https://religion.fandom.com/wiki/Marmoutier_Abbey_(Tours 18.11.2021

12 https://www.britannica.com/biography/Saint-Martin-of-Tours 18.11.2021

13https://commons.wikimedia.org/wiki/File:Vitrail_Saint_Martin_Arc-en-Barrois_281008_1.jpg – https://creativecommons.org/licenses/by-sa/3.0/deed.en - CC BY-SA 3., Vassil 29.01.2022

14 **Stuart, J.** (1869). *The Book of Deer.* Spalding Club : Aberdeen

15 http://www.undiscoveredscotland.co.uk/whithorn/whithornpriory/index.htm 17.10.2020

16 _https://whithorn.info/history/st-ninian-early-christianity-whithorn/ 18.06.2019

17 **Simpson, W.D.** (1925). *The Coming of Christianity in Aberdeenshire.* D. Wyllie & Son : Aberdeen

18 https://commons.wikimedia.org/wiki/File:St.Ninian.dedications.jpg – https://creativecommons.org/licenses/by-sa/3.0/deed.en - CC BY-SA 3., Notuncurious 21.11.2021

19 http://www.cushnieent.com/saints/stdrostan.html 13.11.2021

20 http://www.cushnieent.com/saints/stdrostan.html 13.11.2021

21 Wood carving from St Drostan's Episcopal Church, Old Deer by kind permission of St. Drostan's Vestry 09.01.2022

22 **Towill, E.S. (**1994). *Saints of Scotland.* St. Andrew Press : Edinburgh. ISNB 0-7152-0678-8

23 http://cushnieent.com/saints/stdrostan.htm 13.11.2021

24 https://www.undiscoveredscotland.co.uk/usbiography/f/saintfergus.html 01.08.2019

25 http://cushnieent.com/saints/stfergus.html_13.11.2021

26 **Orem, RD., Martin, PF., Neighbour, RD., McKean, CA., Neighbour, T & Cathcart, A.** (2010). *Historic Fraserburgh : Archeology and development.* Historic Scotland : Edinburgh. ISBN 978-1-902771-79-3 St Modan

27 **Cranna, J**. (1914). *Fraserburgh : Past & Present.* The Rosemount Press : Aberdeen

28 **Murison, D. & Noble, L.** (1995). *Names and Places : A history of place and street names in and around Fraserburgh.* Buchan Publishing **:** Rathen. ISBN 0 9527250 0 2

29 http://cushnieent.com/saints/stcolm.html 13.11.2021

30 http://cushnieent.com/saints/stcolm.html 13.11.2021

31 **Brown, L.J., Martin, A.K., Melville, M.W.** (2021). Map showing Portmahomack in relation to Old Deer

32 **Carver, M.** (2008). *Portmahomack : Monastery of the Picts.* Edinburgh University Press : Edinburgh. ISNB 798 0 7486 2442

33 Artist's impression of a Pictish monastery by kind permission of Lesley Jennings 24.10.2021

34 http://eprints.whiterose.ac.uk/1830/1/carverm2.pdf 15.10.2019

35 http://www.saintsandstones.net/saints-papilstone-journey.html 25.11.20

Chapter 3 – The Book of Deer – The Gospels

1 Author's photograph

2 https://cudl.lib.cam.ac.uk/view/MS-II-00006-00032/ *Cambridge University report.* passim 10.09.2019

3 **Ellsworth, R. & Ellis, P.B.** ((1994). *The Book of Deer.* Constable : London ISBN 0 09 471210 8

4 https://en.wikipedia.org/wiki/Bookbinding#Origins_of_the_book 06.01.2020

5 https://en.wikipedia.org/wiki/Synoptic_Gospels#The_synoptic_problem 24.09.2019

6 https://www.britannica.com/topic/Gospel-According-to-John 24.09.2019

7 http://www.codexsinaiticus.org/en 24.09.2019

8 https://commons.wikimedia.org/wiki/File:Codex_of_Sinay.jpg https://creativecommons.org/licenses/by-sa/3.0/deed.en - CC BY-SA 3. Testus 26.11.2021

9 https://commons.wikimedia.org/wiki/F le:Codex_Vercellensis_-_Old_Latin_gospel_(John_ch._16,_v._23-30)_(The_S.S._Teacher%27s_Edition-The_Holy_Bible_-_Plate_XXXII).jpg Llywrc 26.11.2021

10 https://en.wikipedia.org/wiki/Vetus_Latina 15.09.2019

11 https://en.wikipedia.org/wiki/Jerome 15.09.2019

12https://commons.wikimedia.org/wiki/File:Gerard_David_-_Saint_Jerome_gg0321_b70.jpg https://creativecommons.org/licenses/by-sa/3.0/deed.en - CC BY-SA 3. Jane 023 26.11.2021

13 https://www.britannica.com/topic/Vulgate 10.08.2019

14 **Lawson, A.** (1896). *A Book of the Parish of Deir*. Aberdeen : Free Press Office

15 **Ellsworth, R. & Ellis, P.B.** ((1994). *The Book of Deer.* Constable : London ISBN 0 09 471210 8

16 https://en.wikipedia.org/wiki/Marginalia 25.01.21

17 **Ellsworth, R. & Ellis, P.B.** ((1994). *The Book of Deer.* Constable : London ISBN 0 09 471210 8

18 **Ellsworth, R. & Ellis, P.B.** ((1994). *The Book of Deer.* Constable : London ISBN 0 09 471210 8

19 https://cudl.lib.cam.ac.uk/view/MS-II-00006-00032/ 10.09.2019

20 https://cudl.lib.cam.ac.uk/view/MS-II-00006-00032/ 10.09.2019

Cambridge University report Bibliography:

Stuart, John, *The Book of Deer* (Edinburgh: 1869)

Jackson, Kenneth Hurlstone, *The Gaelic notes in the Book of Deer* (Cambridge: Cambridge University Press, 1972) ISBN: 0521082641 9780521082648

Hughes, Kathleen and D. N. Dumville, *Celtic Britain in the early Middle Ages : studies in Scottish and Welsh sources* (Woodbridge, Suffolk; Totowa, N.J.: Boydell Press ; Rowman & Littlefield, 1980) ISBN: 0847667715 9780847667710 0851151272 9780851151274

Marner, Dominic, "The sword of the spirit, the word of God and the Book of Deer", *Medieval Archaeology* vol. 46 pp. 1-28 (2002)

Geddes, Jane, "The art of the Book of Deer", *Proceedings of the Society of Antiquaries of Scotland* vol. 128 pp. 537-549 (1998)

Henderson, I., "Abstracts: the Book of Deer", in International Congress of Celtic Studies , *Proceedings of the Seventh International Congress of Celtic Studies held at Oxford, from 10th to 15th July, 1983* contributor: D. Ellis Evans contributor: John Griffith contributor: E. M. Jope (Oxford: D.E. Evans, 1986)

Studies on the Book of Deer contributor: **Katherine Forsyth** (Dublin: Four Courts Press, 2008) ISBN: 185182569X

21 **Geddes, Jane,** (1998). *The art of the Book of Deer.* IN Proceedings of the Society of Antiquaries of Scotland. Vol. 128 pp. 537-549

22 Aberdeenshire Council Historic Environment Record - Moray - NJ26SW0474 - THE ELGIN PILLAR 20.07.2021

23 **Stuart, John** (1856). *Sculptured stones of Scotland.* The Spalding Club : Aberdeen

23 **Geddes, Jane,** (1998). *The art of the Book of Deer.* IN Proceedings of the Society of Antiquaries of Scotland. Vol. 128 pp. 537-549

24 https://blog.nms.ac.uk/2015/05/27/glenmorangie-research-project-monymusk-reliquary 20.01.2020

25 **Geddes, Jane,** (1998). *The art of the Book of Deer.* IN Proceedings of the Society of Antiquaries of Scotland. Vol. 128 pp. 537-549

26 https://commons.wikimedia.org/wiki/File:The_Monymusk_Reliquary_(8652807884).jpg https://creativecommons.org/licenses/by-sa/2.0/deed.en - CC BY-SA 2., Fae 20.10.2021

27https://commons.wikimedia.org/wiki/File:The_Pictish_penannular_silver_bowls_in_the_hoard_from_St_Ninian%27s_Isle,_Shetland.jpg https://creativecommons.org/licenses/by-sa/4.0/deed.en - CC BY-SA 4. Adamcoulson 11.11.2021

28 https://commons.wikimedia.org/wiki/File:Box_holy_oils_Louvre_OA6935.jpg https://creativecommons.org/licenses/by-sa/3.0/deed.en - CC BY-SA 3., Soerfm/Marie-Lan Nguyen (2006) 26.11.2021

29 https://commons.wikimedia.org/wiki/File:Coffret_aux_saintes_huiles,_%C3%A9tain_-_%C3%89glise_de_Thorign%C3%A9-en-Charnie.jpg https://creativecommons.org/licenses/by-sa/3.0/deed.en - CC BY-SA 3. Symac / Sylvain Machefert 01.11.2021

30 https://en.wikipedia.org/wiki/Old_Roman_Symbol 20.01.2020

31 https://www.britannica.com/art/colophon-visual-art 01.02.2020

32 **Kellock, A.** (c. 2010). *This Splendid Little Book*. The Book of Deer Project : Mintlaw (Leaflet)

33 **Stuart, J.** (Ed.) (1869). *The Book of Deer.* Spalding Club : Edinburgh

34 **Kellock, A.** (c. 2010). *This Splendid Little Book*. The Book of Deer Project : Mintlaw (Leaflet)

35 **Geddes, Jane,** (1998). *The art of the Book of Deer.* IN Proceedings of the Society of Antiquaries of Scotland. Vol. 128 pp. 537-549

36 http//www./medievalchronicles.com/medieval-art/illuminated-manuscripts/ 15.09.2019

37 **Stuart, J.** (1856). *Sculptured Stones of Scotland.* Spalding Club : Aberdeen

38 **Stuart, J.** (1856). *Sculptured Stones of Scotland.* Spalding Club : Aberdeen

39https://blog.europeana.eu/2019/01/lighting-the-way-how-illuminated-initials-guided-medieval-readers-through-books 04.05.2020

40 https://earlychurchhistory.org/christian-symbols/the-chi-rho-symbol 10.02.2021

41 https://commons.wikimedia.org/wiki/File:Simple_Labarum.svg https://creativecommons.org/licenses/by-sa/public_domain/deed.en - CC BY-SA Public_Domai Aethralis 02.12.2021

42 https://en.wikipedia.org/wiki/Chi_Rho 05.05.2020

43 https://medievalbooks.nl/2018/10/05/doodles-in-medieval-manuscripts 03.02.2020

44 **Henderson, I.** (2008), *Understanding the figurative style and decorative programme of the Book of Deer.* IN Forsyth. K. (Ed.) Studies on the Book of Deer. Four Courts Press Ltd. : Dublin. ISBN. 978 – 1 – 85182 – 1

45 **Stuart, J.** (Ed.) (1869). *The Book of Deer.* Spalding Club : Edinburgh

46 **Lawson, A.** (1896). *A Book of the Parish of Deir*. Aberdeen : Free Press Office

47 **Stuart, J.** (Ed.) (1869). *The Book of Deer.* Spalding Club : Edinburgh

48 https://www.publicdomainpictures.net/en/view-image.php?image=177465&picture=river-otter-swimming 12.07.2021

49 **Stuart, J.** (Ed.) (1869). *The Book of Deer.* Spalding Club : Edinburgh

50 https://en.wikipedia.org/wiki/St_Ninian%27s_Isl 08.03.2020

51 https://commons.wikimedia.org/wiki/File:St_Ninian%27s_Isle_TreasureDSCF6209.jpg https://creativecommons.org/licenses/by-sa/3.0/deed.en - CC BY-SA 3., Johnbod 02.12.2021

52 https://commons.wikimedia.org/wiki/File:St_Ninian%27s_Isle_TreasureDSCF6202det.jpg https://creativecommons.org/licenses/by-sa/3.0/deed.en - CC BY-SA 3. Johnbod 02.12.2021

53 https://commons.wikimedia.org/wiki/File:Replica_of_the_Deskford_Carnyx_(9487528587).jpg https://creativecommons.org/licenses/by-sa/2.0/deed.en - CC BY-SA 2. Lirazelf 02.12.2021

54 **Elsworth, R, & Ellis P.B.** (1994). *The Book of Deer.* Constable & Co. Ltd. : London ISBN 0-09-473210-8

55 **Bible** https://en.wikipedia.org/wiki/Epistle_of_James#Anointing_of_the_Sic 31.01.2020

56 **Markus, G.** (2008). The sick and dying in the Book of Deer. IN Forsyth, K. (Ed.) *Studies on The Book of Deed. r.* Four Courts Press : Dublin, ISBN 978-1-85182-569-1. pp 67-97

57 **Dominic Marner** (2002) *The Sword of the Spirit, the Word of God and the Book of Deer,* Medieval Archaeology, 46:1, 1-28, DOI: 10.1179/med.2002.46.1. 03 05 2020

58 **Markus, G.** (2008). The sick and dying in the Book of Deer. IN Forsyth, K. (Ed.) *Studies on The Book of Deer.* Four Courts Press : Dublin, ISBN 978-1-85182-569-1. pp 67-97

59 **Stuart, J.** (Ed.) (1869). *The Book of Deer.* Spalding Club : Edinburgh

60 **Markus, G.** (2008). The sick and dying in the Book of Deer. IN Forsyth, K. (Ed.) *Studies on The Book of Deer.* Four Courts Press : Dublin, ISBN 978-1-85182-569-1. pp 67-97

61 https://en.wikipedia.org/wiki/Mozarabic_Rit 4.12.2020

62 https://en.wikipedia.org/wiki/Gallican_Rit 4.12.2020

Chapter 4 – The Book of Deer – Later Entries

1 **Woolf, A.** (2000). *The "Moray Question" and the Kingship of Alba in the Tenth and Eleventh Centuries.* The Scottish Historical Review Vol. LXXIX,2 No.208 October 2000. 145-164

2 https://en.wikipedia.org/wiki/Saint_Margaret_of_Scotland 08.12.2019

3 **Ellsworth, R. & Ellis, P.** (1994). *The Book of Deer.* Constable & Co. : London. ISBN 0-009-473210-8

4 **Jackson, K.** (1972). *The Gaelic Notes in the Book of Deer.* Cambridge University Press : Cambridge. ISNB 978 0 521 08464 1.

5 **Marcus, G.** (2008). *The Sick and Dying in the Book of Deer.* IN Forsyth, K. (2008). Studies on the Book of Deer. Four Court Press : Dublin. JSBN 978 1851825691

6 **Duncan, A.A.M.** (1975). *Scotland The Making of a Kingdom.* Oliver & Boyd : Edinburgh. ISBN 0 05 003183 X

7 https://celt.ucc.ie/published/G102007.html 08.12.2019

8 **Jackson, K.** (1972). *The Gaelic Notes in the Book of Deer.* Cambridge University Press : Cambridge. ISNB 978 0 521 08464 1

9 **Duncan, A.A.M.** (1975). *Scotland The Making of a Kingdom.* Oliver & Boyd : Edinburgh. ISBN 0 05 003183 X

10https://forestryandland.gov.scot/images/corporate/pdf/the-picts-a-learning-resource 08.05.2020

11 **Woolf A.** (2000). The 'Moray Question' and the Kingship of Alba in the Tenth and Eleventh Centuries. IN *The Scottish historical Review. Vol.LXXIX. 2. No.208 October 2000, 145 – 164.* https://www.academia.edu/313148/ TheMoray_Questionand_the_Kingship_of_Alba_in_the_Tenth_and_Eleventh_Centurie 20 01 2020. Passim

12 **Stuart, J.** (Ed.) (1869). *The Book of Deer.* The Spalding Club Aberdeen

13. **Macbain, A.** (1885) The Book of Deer. IN *Transactions of the Gaelic Society of Inverness* Vol.XI 1884 – 85. R. Carruthers & Sons : Inverness

14 **Jackson, K.** (1972). *The Gaelic Notes in the Book of Deer.* Cambridge University Press : Cambridge. ISNB 978 0 521 08464 1.

15 **Woolf A.** (2000). The 'Moray Question' and the Kingship of Alba in the Tenth and Eleventh Centuries. IN *The Scottish historical Review. Vol.LXXIX. 2. No.208 October 2000, 145 – 164.* https://www.academia.edu/313148/ TheMoray_Questionand_the_Kingship_of_Alba_in_the_Tenth_and_Eleventh_Centurie 20 01 2020. passim

16 **Jackson, K.** (1972). *The Gaelic Notes in the Book of Deer.* Cambridge University Press : Cambridge. ISNB 978 0 521 08464 1

17 **Macbain, A.** (1885) *The Book of Deer.* IN Transactions of the Gaelic Society of Inverness. Vol.XI 1884 – 85. R. Carruthers & Sons : Inverness

18 **Woolf, A.** (2000). *The "Moray Question" and the Kingship of Alba in the Tenth and Eleventh Centuries.* The Scottish Historical Review Vol. LXXIX,2 No.208 October 2000. 145-164

19 https://www.sizes.com/units/davoch.html 22.11.2021

20 https://everipedia.org/wiki/lang_en/Macbeth,_King_of_Scotland 09.03.2020

21 **Macbain, A.** (1885) The Book of Deer. IN *Transactions of the Gaelic Society of Inverness.* Vol.XI 1884 – 85. R. Carruthers & Sons : Inverness

22 ibid.

23 ibid.

24 **Jackson, K.** (1972). *The Gaelic Notes in the Book of Deer.* Cambridge University Press : Cambridge. ISNB 978 0 521 08464 1

25 https://en.wikipedia.org/wiki/Earl_of_Buchan 30.05.2019

26 https://en.wikipedia.org/wiki/Nechtan_of_Aberdeen 11.05.2020

27https://en.wikipedia.org/wiki/Bishop_of_Brechin 22.11.2021

28 **Brown, L.J., Martin, A.K., Melville, M.W.** (2022). Photograph of Moot Hill Memorial in Ellon beside the Ythan

29https://commons.wikimedia.org/wiki/
File:Malcolm_IV,_King_of_Scotland,_charter_to_Kelso_Abbey,_1159,_initial_(crop_David_I).jpg
https://creativecommons.org/licenses/in the public domain User-duck 20.11.2021

30 **Duncan, A.A.M.** (1975). *Scotland The Making of a Kingdom :The Edinburgh History of Scotland* Vol. I. Oliver & Boyd : Edinburgh. ISBN. 0 05 003183 X. passim

31 **Jackson, K.** (1972). *The Gaelic Notes in the Book of Deer.* Cambridge University Press : Cambridge. ISNB 978 0 521 08464 1

32 **Cramond, W.** (1893). *The Annals of Banff.* New Spalding Club : Aberdeen

33 https://en.wikipedia.org/wiki/Urquhart%2C_Mora 26.03.2020

34 www.ucc.ie/research/celt/published/G102007.html 15.12.2019

35https://books.google.co.uk/books?
id=9G8AAAAAMAAJ&pg=PA73&lpg=PA73&dq=Gregory+Bishop+of+Dunkeld&source=bl&ots=nLaWdXTpAS&sig=ACfU3U39_FvcOMd0O28gzuYM4sFQibxE2w 15.12.2019

36 https://en.wikipedia.org/wiki/Aindr%C3%A9as_of_Caithness 15.12.2019

37 https://en.wikipedia.org/wiki/Bishop_of_Brechin 11.05.2020

38 https://en.wikipedia.org/wiki/Donnchad_I,_Earl_of_Fife 16.12.2019

39 https://en.wikipedia.org/wiki/M%C3%A1el_Muire,_Earl_of_Atholl 16.12.2019

40 https://en.wikipedia.org/wiki/Gille_Brigte,_Earl_of_Angus 16.12.2019

41 **Jackson, K.** (1972). *The Gaelic Notes in the Book of Deer.* Cambridge University Press : Cambridge. ISNB 978 0 521 08464 1

42 **Brown, L.J., Martin, A.K., Melville, M.W.** (2021). Map showing lands granted to the Monastery of Deer. 13.02.2022

43 **Jackson, K.** (1972). *The Gaelic Notes in the Book of Deer.* Cambridge University Press : Cambridge. ISNB 978 0 521 08464 1

44 **Brown, L.J., Martin, A.K., Melville, M.W.** (2021). Map showing possible additions of lancs granted to the Monastery of Deer 13.02.2022

45 **Taylor, S.** (2008). *The toponymic landscape of the Gaelic Notes in the Book of Deer* IN Forsyth, K. (Ed.) *Studies on the Book of Deer.* Four Courts Press Ltd. : Dublin ISBN 978-1-85182-569-1

46 **Pratt, J.B.** (1901). *Buchan.* 4th Ed. Lewis Smith and Son : Aberdeen

47 **Gray, J.** (1894). Paper on the Personal and Place Names in the Book of Deer, IN *Transactions of the Buchan Field Club* (1892—95). Vol. 3 Buchan Field Club : Peterhead.

48 **Stuart, J.** (Ed.) (1869). *The Book of Deer.* The Spalding Club : Aberdeen

Chapter 5 – The Monastery of Turriff

1 **Milne, J.** (1890a) *'The early history of Turriff', Trans. Banffshire Field Club, 1889-90.* Page(s): 12-17, 22

2 **Warren, F. E**. The liturgy and ritual of the Celtic Church https://www.google.co.uk/books/edition/The_Liturgy_and_Ritual_of_the_Celtic_Chu/1YZbAAAAMAAJ?hl=en&gbpv=1&printsec=frontcover

3 **Milne, J.** (1890a) *'The early history of Turriff', Trans Banffshire Field Club, 1889-90.* Page(s): 12-17, 22

4 **Stuart, J.** (Ed.) (1869). *The Book of Deer.* The Spalding Club : Aberdeen

5 **Pratt, J B**. (1901). *Buchan* 4th Ed. Lewis Smith & Son : Aberdeen

6 **W. Douglas Simpson** (1935). *The Celtic Church in Scotland* pp 84-85

7 **Stuart, J.** (Ed.) (1869). *The Book of Deer.* The Spalding Club : Aberdeen

8 **Simpson, W.D.** (1935). *The Celtic Church in Scotland* pp 84-85

9 **Milne, J.** (1890a) *'The early history of Turriff', Trans Banffshire Field Club, 1889-90.* Page(s): 12-17, 22

10 https://www.shetlandamenity.org/archaeology-collection-awarded-status-of-national-significance

11 **Garner H.W**. (2007). *St. Congan in Historical Perspective : A Celtic Saint of the Isles, The Highlands and Aberdeenshire.* http//www.amazon.co.uk-Congan-Hiatorical Perspective-Highlands-Aberdeenshire/dp/0955383706 03 03 2021

12 **Milne, J.** (1890a) *'The early history of Turriff', Trans Banffshire Field Club, 1889-90.* Page(s): 12-17, 22

13 **Stuart, John** (1856). *Sculptured stones of Scotland.* The Spalding Club : Aberdeen

14 **Stuart, J.** (Ed.) (1869). *The Book of Deer.* The Spalding Club : Aberdeen

15 **Jackson, K.** (1972). *The Gaelic Notes in the Book of Deer.* Cambridge University Press : Cambridge. ISBN 0 521 08264 3

16 https://celt.ucc.ie/published/G102007.html 17.06.2020

17 **Jackson, K.** (1972). *The Gaelic Notes in the Book of Deer.* Cambridge University Press : Cambridge. ISBN 0 521 08264 3

18 **Milne, J.** (1890a) *'The early history of Turriff', Trans Banffshire Field Club, 1889-90.* Page(s): 12-17, 22

19 **Stuart, J.** (1866). *Notice of the Church of St. Congan in Aberdeenshire.* Proceedings of the Society : May 1866

20 https://celt.ucc.ie/published/G102007.html 20.06.2020

21 https://www.poms.ac.uk/record/factoid/46109/ People of Medieval Scotland 20.06.2020

22 https://celt.ucc.ie/published/G102007.html 20.06.2020

23 https://www.poms.ac.uk/record/person/755/ People of Medieval Scotland 28.11.2021

24 **Milne, J.** (1890a) *'The early history of Turriff', Trans Banffshire Field Club, 1889-90.* Page(s): 12-17, 22

25 **Simpson, D.S.** (1923). *The Origins of Christianity in Aberdeenshire.* Wyllie & Son : Aberdeen.

26 https://en.wikipedia.org/wiki/Feudalism#Classic_feudalism 21.05.2021

27 http://www2.thesetonfamily.com:8080/history/History_1.htm 28.11.2021

28 https://en.wikipedia.org/wiki/Mormaer 21.05.21

29 **Duncan, A.A.M.** (1975). *Scotland : The Making of a Kingdom.* Oliver & Boyd : Edinburgh. ISBN 0 05 003183 X

30 https://en.wikipedia.org/wiki/Marjory,_Countess_of_Buchan 11.05.2021

31 **Duncan, A.A.M.** (1975). *Scotland : The Making of a Kingdom.* Oliver & Boyd : Edinburgh. ISBN 0 05 003183 X

32 **Melville, M.W.** (2008). *Deer Abbey.* The Book of Deer Project : Maud

33 https://stataccscot.edina.ac.uk/static/statacc/dist/essay/boundaries 28.11.2021

34 https://www.poms.ac.uk/record/source/2612/ 12.03.2021

35 https://www.aberdeenshire.gov.uk/media/24934/2018-08-14-historic-churches-webready-v3_a3-searchable.pdf 21.05.21

36 The remains of St Congan's Church, Turriff. Photograph by kind permission of L.J. Brown

37 **Stuart, J.** (Ed.) (1869). *The Book of Deer.* The Spalding Club : Aberdeen